How to Find Your Vocation

'**How to Find Your Vocation** is certainly a book to which I shall return again and again in my encouragement of vocations, not only to the ordained ministry, but to the lay vocation in the world. The quotations are a veritable goldmine.'

Michael Turnbull, Bishop of Durham

'This is an extremely important book. It pours itself as a bright light into a world of work that has become much riddled with disillusionment, insecurity, fear, helplessness and inevitability . . . It doesn't have to be like this. Drawing on a lifetime's observation and reflection, John Adair has written a book that is filled with new hope; not just for individuals but also for organisations and commercial enterprises. There is a prophetically statesman-like quality to the quiet call to re-think vocation for corporate bodies, but this follows much that is addressed to the individual.'

European Review, Spring 2001

John Adair is an internationally renowned author and consultant on leadership and management. His twenty-seven books, including the best-selling *Effective Leadership* and *How to Manage Your Time* have sold over a million copies and have been translated into fourteen languages.

He has taught at Oxford, Surrey and Exeter Universities; he was the first Director of Studies at St George's House, Windsor, and has also been adviser to the Archbishops' Council of the Church of England. He lives near Guildford.

How to Find Your Vocation

A guide to discovering the work you love

John Adair

CANTERBURY
PRESS
Norwich

First hardback edition published in 2000 by
The Canterbury Press Norwich
(a publishing imprint of Hymns Ancient & Modern Limited
a registered charity)
St. Mary's Works, St. Mary's Plain
Norwich, Norfolk, NR3 3BH

This paperback edition published in 2002

British Library Cataloguing in Publication Data

A catalogue record for this book is available
from the British Library

ISBN 1-85311-416-1

Typeset by Rowland Phototypesetting Ltd,
Bury St Edmunds, Suffolk
and printed in Great Britain by
Biddles Ltd, *www.biddles.co.uk*

Contents

For Thea

Preface

Blessed is the man who has found his vocation: let him ask for nothing more.

John Ruskin

Blessed indeed! But how can you find *your* vocation? That question must have been considered either irrelevant to life or impossible to answer, because, amazingly, I cannot discover any other book that has ever been written on the subject. There are, of course, some academic studies on vocation written from theological standpoints, and for that matter a growing secular literature on the spirituality of work, but I can find no down-to-earth practical guide on how – if at all – you can actually discover your calling in life. So here goes!

First, please check to see if you are on the right railway train. Is this the right book for you? Vocation is a confusing word, and so I should say 'up-front' what I mean by it.

In English, vocation is used *generally* of careers, as in such phrases as 'vocational training', 'vocational guidance' and 'national vocational qualifications'. It is also used of *particular professions*, such as those followed by priests, nuns, monks, missionaries and – not so frequently now – of other so-called caring professions such as doctors, nurses and teachers.

Linguistically, the concept of vocation seems to be like a fading star; emitting ever less light as it recedes into the constellation of organized religion, seeming to move ever further away from real life. The ascendant star in this galaxy is of course *career*. Indeed *vocation* is virtually reduced to being not much more than one of the satellite synonyms, like *profession*, *craft* or *trade*, that once shone before slipping away into the oblivion of archaisms.

So it's certainly difficult! Present usage leads us to think of vocation *either* as merely career by another name *or* as a divine summons to a special course of life and as a label for that course – specifically for a religious (if not Christian) occupation or state. We are pushed by our present usage of the term into that futile dichotomy. You can see the dilemma I have to struggle with.

On the one hand, it would be pointless writing another book on choosing and managing your own career – there are plenty of those available. On the other hand, if vocations are only religious, how can people be said to *find* them? Rather it seems as if vocation finds them. In their cases, I agree with the American writer John Jay Chapman: 'If their vocation is real,' he wrote, 'it will vanquish all obstacles and will stand out, not as a mere invitation but as a categorical imperative.' Not much market for a book there!

As you may have guessed, I am heading on a middle course between this Scylla and Charybdis. Why not see vocation not in these stark black-or-white, either/or terms, but as a *spectrum* of possibilities? There are a number of stations on this line and perhaps one of them is the right station stop for you.

People choose careers for different motives. Many seem to be guided by one factor only: which pays the most. Now if becoming rich is your chief and unalterable criterion for career choice, you are definitely on the wrong train: we are still standing at the station, so there's time to get off!

If you 'have a vocation' in the religious sense, or if some angel has already whispered in your ear what to do with your life, then these pages probably won't be much help to you either. Your train has already departed and your spirit is on it.

So, those of us who are left, where are we going? I am assuming now that you are seeking something more in life than just a job, however well paid. And I am assuming, too, that you don't necessarily have a 'vocation' in the Church sense, or perhaps you do and you would like to understand more of what is propelling you forward. After all, even religious vocations turn out to be mistaken sometimes.

Because I am committed to taking you into the unknown middle ground of the vocational spectrum, this book cannot be just tips or hints on how to choose a satisfying career. The concept of vocation or calling implies a sense of something or someone *other* than yourself which is doing the calling. That may or may not be illusory, but it is how people talk about vocation.

Now I could call that *other* by names of various related sorts, the chief of which in English is God. But I want to avoid that as much as I can, because for people who don't define themselves as religious it is a name that carries too many over-tones of faith. Yet whatever the name used or unused, *that* is the experience I hope that you will have. Maybe not when you shut the book. Yet there are seeds of thoughts on the pages which, falling into your mind, may contribute to leading you eventually to a place where you seem to be saying yes.

In one sense the unfolding of your vocation is a complete mystery. No one can say when, where or how that discovery of your vocation will happen. But in another sense, it is equally true that vocation is not a mystery at all. As Albert Einstein said, 'God does not play dice with us.' If a great scientist is patient and persevering, he or she eventually finds what they are searching for – a universal principle or law relating the apparently unconnected phenomena. In this context, what is that universal principle? I suggest that it is this: *If you fulfil the necessary conditions, as dawn follows night, your vocation will be revealed to you.*

But *necessary conditions* are not the same as the *sufficient condition* – that which is required for it to happen. Let me use a simple analogy. You build of pile of sticks and newspaper on a dry day and then put a match to it. Your preparations and the weather are necessary conditions, for without them –

no fire. The struck and applied match is the sufficient condition – a touch of flame, a blazing fire.

In that analogy, however, you control both the conditions. In vocation all you can do is to build the mound of wood: whether or not it is ignited and becomes a fire is not at your command. You cannot *cause* the effect, but you can *invite* it. Artists often say much the same about inspiration.

A hundred experiments in science do not prove the truth of a theory, only that – so far – it has withstood tests to disprove it. Yet one experiment can falsify it.

So here is your challenge! See if *you* can prove me wrong! Fulfil the necessary conditions as described in this book, including patience, then wait and see if vocation comes to you.

If I was a betting man I would wager a very large sum that it will work, that you will find your vocation – or it will find you. But it isn't an absolute law of cause-and-effect; nor is there any guarantee of a favourable response, or even a response at all. For we are not dealing with an automaton but with something or someone as free and potentially capricious as we are ourselves.

Why, then, am I so confidence that it will happen? Because somewhere buried in the necessary conditions – exactly where or how I don't know – is an offer that the *other* cannot refuse. The universal law of reciprocity – giving evokes an equal or greater giving in response – kicks into action, just as it does in our human webs of exchange. As the Spanish proverb vividly puts it: 'Take what you want,' says God. 'Take it and pay for it.'

Vocations which we wanted to pursue but did not, bleed like colours in the whole of our experience.

Balzac

I

Some Characteristics of
Vocational People

*When men are rightly occupied, their amusement
grows out of their work, as the colour-petals out of
a fruitful flower.*

John Ruskin

One way of understanding what vocation means is to look at
people who seem to have found their vocations. What attributes and values do they have in common – if any?

Remember that I am not suggesting that the world divides into
the fortunate few who 'have a vocation' and the rest. On the
contrary, I believe passionately that the door that leads to
vocation is open to us all. So I see this chapter as more a step
towards clarifying what we mean by vocation, and as a way of
encouraging you to see it more as a spectrum – not as something
you either have or not and there's nothing you can do about it.
You can do a great deal to attract this blessing into your life.

Vocation is not restricted to a limited number of people,
such as artists or composers. They are merely examples of
a much more universal phenomenon. Vocational people are
widespread in most societies, more so in some than others. For
culture, religion and education – that inseparable trinity – are
significant factors in their emergence. The hypothesis that
vocation is much more common than is often imagined can be
easily tested.

You will need some paper and something to write with at

this point. For what I should like you to do is to jot down some answers to this simple question:

Exercise

Think of the people that you know, have read about or seen on television whom you consider to be vocational in the sense that they appear to be in just the right walk of life, so that you can hardly imagine them doing anything else. Try to identify at least five of them and put their names down. Next, what do you consider to be the principal characteristics that these people have in common? Make a list.

You can widen the exercise, if you like, by asking friends or colleagues the same questions. I have done this myself and, even allowing for similar words and phrases, have ended up with quite a long list of characteristics.

What I have done in this chapter is to select nine attributes and values – some of them overlapping – which seem to be the key ones. You may like to compare your list in answer to the question above with mine. I should be surprised if we don't have some of the characteristics in common, which suggests that there *is* such a thing as the phenomenon of vocation, however you may choose to explain it.

It is worth looking at my whole list first, in order to gain an impression of what a person who is more towards the vocational end of the spectrum is like. Then I will reflect briefly on each of the characteristics in turn.

Some Key Vocational Characteristics

1. Dedication

Vocational people are most noticeable for the dedication or commitment they show in the daily lives and work. This is usually accompanied by self-discipline.

2. 'Fit'

Their interests, aptitudes and temperament appear to be in balance with the needs and requirements of their work. It breeds a level of self-confidence.

3. Not for Money Alone

Although vocational people may like money and become wealthy they are not materially minded: in the last resort they do not work for pay or financial gain.

4. Creativity

Creativity takes many different forms, ranging from artistic creativity to the creativity which people exhibit in social life, for example by creating a human enterprise out of an idea.

5. Enthusiasm

Work becomes for vocational people their principal source of enjoyment or fun. They are invariably enthusiastic if not passionate about what they are doing.

6. Humility

Humility stems from the sense of being a servant to the work, and through the work to larger and more important purposes than self. It is not the denial of self, but the absence of self-importance.

7. Tenacity

Vocational people do not give up easily, which is as well because the path of vocation is seldom an easy one.

8. Service

If they are not 'in it for the money', what motivates vocational people? Many exhibit a strong sense of service. In some contexts that amounts to serving individuals, in others it takes one of the many forms of public service. But the service-orientation is unmistakeable.

9. Love

At its simplest, vocational people have found the work they love to do. They may use the word *love* in conversation about their work or some aspect of it. They are extremely reluctant to give it up.

I am not suggesting that all vocational people have all these characteristics or manifest all these values, or that – when present – they are there in equal measure, but there is usually a 'critical mass' of these qualities, each on a continuum of relative strength. And so we are looking more for a pattern than for individual characteristics as such. In other words, a person might have one or two of these characteristics – tenacity, for example – and still not feel himself or herself to be a vocational person.

1. Dedication

The most common characteristic of vocational people is their sense of dedication to their art, craft or profession. If you want to spot a vocational person this is the first thing to look for.

The eminent founder and conductor of Scottish Opera, Sir Alexander Gibson, was once asked in a press interview about the sources of his philosophy of life. He replied:

A quote from Rachmaninov has from time to time reassured me that it is not altogether unhealthy to be obsessed with one subject – sometimes to the exclusion of all other concerns and aspect of life:

> *I am myself only in music,*
> *Music is enough for a whole lifetime –*
> *But a lifetime is not enough for music.*

So I suppose my general philosophy of life consists of accepting the fact that music means more to me than any other facet of life and I count myself indeed fortunate that it can be my relaxation as well as my occupation, my consolation in times of stress and my inspiration in facing up to the vicissitudes of life.

I am also fortunate in having a wife and four children who accept this state of affairs and back me up without question or reservation.

I read scores for relaxation – especially scores of music I don't have to prepare for an imminent performance – but I also read books, mostly history and biography.

Generally, however, I am myself only in music and I believe almost Calvinistically, especially as a conductor who depends upon others who in turn are largely dependent on him, that a conductor's work is never done. There are always new scores to learn but I find I spend more and more time on the scores I think I have known for decades. No lifetime is long enough for a servant of music, but I never cease to wonder at the achievement of the composers whose lifespans were so tragically short. It is indeed a privilege to serve all of them by being involved in the process which keeps their music alive.

Notice that sense of being privileged to serve music and others in it – the great composers and one's colleagues in the orchestra. Seeing one's work as a form of service is a theme I shall return to later.

Dedication is a word with religious overtones. It derives from the solemn ceremonies by which a temple was consecrated for sacred use. To be dedicated means, then, to feel or act as if you have been set apart for some particular noble or sacred end.

Nowadays we tend to use the word 'commitment' more often than dedication, possibly because it doesn't convey those religious overtones. From the French we derive our word *engagement*, which carries the sense of binding oneself to do something, accepting a legal or moral obligation.

Vocational people are drawn to being committed sometimes long before they discovery what to commit themselves to. That is partly what I mean by implying that there is a distinction between being a vocational person and finding your vocation. For I believe that the seeds or potential for all nine characteristics are in us all. In varying degrees most of us *need* and seek a purpose in life worthy of our devotion. For some the need for devotion to something outside oneself is even stronger than the need for companionship. Most of us, mercifully, don't have to make that choice.

One of the first questions to ask yourself in your quest for your vocation, then, is: 'Am I willing to commit myself completely to something beyond or other than the sole pursuit of self-interest?' I am not asking you to sign a blank cheque – yet. But that willingness has to be there – it is a necessary condition. At some time later you may convert it into commitment and become, in William Wordsworth's phrase, a 'dedicated Spirit'. Your life is never quite your own.

Dedication is not something that vocational people tend to talk about; they tend not to be self-conscious people anyway. They wear their total commitment lightly, often with a smile. But dedication is the steel behind the smile. Its presence is revealed in the willingness to go the extra mile, to serve others in spirit well beyond the letter of the contract, and to do what needs to be done – not what one is paid to do. As the French proverb says: '*He gives nothing who does not give himself.*'

Once Michelangelo, painting frescoes in the Sistine Chapel, was lying on his back on a high scaffold, carefully outlining a figure in a corner of the ceiling. A friend asked him why he took such pains with a figure that would be many feet away from the viewer.

'After all,' said the friend, 'who will know whether it is perfect or not?'

'I will,' said the artist.

A Vocational Person

As I was about to start writing this chapter I read about a tragic accident in which a young doctor bled to death at her remote holiday cottage after falling from a ladder and severing a main artery. Dr Alison Bell, 37, had just been appointed as a consultant in geriatrics at my local hospital, the Royal Surrey at Guildford. She had trained at St Bartholomew's and was working on a pioneering drug for the elderly. The medical director said:

'Even in a profession where you deal with death on an almost daily basis this has hit everyone very hard. She just seemed so young. She was a delightful girl, very unassuming. The patients were enormously fond of her. Alison was totally dedicated to them. The job was her life. She lived for it and loved it. She worked with a quiet precision and was very popular with patients and staff. She will be greatly missed by everyone.'

It is evident that Alison had found her true vocation. She had also recently taken a step upwards on the ladder of her medical career. For her vocation and career were moving together hand-in-hand, only to be cancelled by a fatal slip on that other ladder. But such people as Alison are the salt of society, and they serve us still as candle-lights of inspiration.

2. 'Fit'

By 'fit' I mean that vocational people seem to be perfectly adapted to the ends they serve. They do not have difficulty in meeting the requirements or demands of their job: in their case it is a matter of 'doing what comes naturally'.

'*No two of us are born exactly alike. We have different aptitudes, which fit us for different jobs,*' wrote Plato in *The Republic*. '*Quantity and quality are therefore more easily produced when a man specializes appropriately on a single job for which he is naturally fitted.'* These are the fundamental principles of vocation, and the fact that Plato enunciated them should guard us against any assumption that the concept of vocation is specifically Christian 'property'. We are dealing with a universal phenomenon. I have emphasized these words in italics because those two principles really are the bedrock or foundation stone of vocation. Those whom we perceive as being vocational people have discovered that optimum balance between society's needs or demands and their (developed) natural abilities. And so work *flows* from them without too much effort, both in terms of quantity and quality.

Perhaps I should have said that vocational people make their work *look* easy, just as the dance of a ballerina looks easy. But considerable dedication lies behind that ease. Plato went on to say, 'The workman must be at the *call* of his job; his job will not wait until he has leisure to spare for it.' For Plato, then, each job or function has its needs, demands, requirements or duties. Responding to the call of the job takes a higher priority that one's own comfort or leisure.

There seems to be no gap for vocational people between what they do and what they are. Gerald Manley Hopkins, the Jesuit poet, echoed this in his poem, 'Kingfishers and Dragonflies', 'What I do is me: for that I came.'

3. Not for Money Alone

In vocational people the nexus between working and getting money for work is a weak one. *Vocation stresses a long-term commitment to something that is not necessarily equated with the earning of a livelihood.* An artist may paint as her vocation, but earn her living as a waitress.

This unconnectedness between vocation and money is obscured by the fact that normally your vocation is also the principal means by which you earn money to support yourself and your family. But a purely mercenary attitude to your work or business is a sure symptom of lack of vocation.

In times past there was a tendency to exploit the dedication of vocational people doing the job they loved. Traditionally, the rates of remuneration of nurses and teachers, for example, have been low. But this is ethically wrong; no one should be allowed to make unjust or improper use of others for their own profit or commercial advantage. Not paying people the market rate for their work is a good example of that. You may be willing to give your services freely – others may indeed ask you to do so for some good cause. But that is quite different from someone else trading on your vocational commitment to your disadvantage.

There is a common tendency these days to elevate financial reward into the supreme motive for work. Internet millionaires and stock market winners are fêted, 'fat-cat' bonuses make the headlines. The message is incessant: 'Everyone else is doing it, why not you?'

The trouble with putting money first is that it eventually drives out of the work place all other satisfactions. Money is like a drug and subject to the law of diminishing returns. You always need more. Gradually, imperceptibly, the enjoyment or fun goes out of work and it becomes a grind, a rat-race to earn even more money. Any sense of the other non-material values that make work interesting, rewarding and worthwhile is lost. 'There is not much money in poetry,' once mused Robert Frost. 'But then there is not much poetry in money either.'

4. Creativity

Vocational people are generally creative. That doesn't mean, as I have said, that they are all artists, composers or writers. There are a thousand different ways of being creative. We tend to think too much in terms of artistic or scientific creativity, and ignore the amazing amount of personal and social creativity all around us, not least in the way that people fulfil their ideas. As Antonio tells his friend in *The Merchant of Venice*:

> I hold the world but as the world, Gratiano,
> A stage where every man must play his part;
> And mine a sad one.

For Shakespeare it must have been natural to see life as a drama – part-comedy, part-tragedy – in which we each play a part. To some extent our *role* (from the French word for the roll upon which an actor's part is written) is assigned to us. For example, we are cast as male or female, older or younger players. Ours may be a major or minor role. But the *way* we interpret it is an expression of creativity, or at least it is so for vocational people. I shall return to this subject later (in Chapter 8), but here are a few preliminary thoughts.

Vocation means having a part in the drama, not being one of life's spectators. To find your vocation is always to be called into the action. The philosopher Immanuel Kant observed:

> It is by his activities and not by enjoyment that man feels that he is alive. The busier we are the more we feel that we live and the more conscious we are of life. In idleness we not only feel that life is fleeting but we also feel lifeless. Activity is a part of life's substance . . . Life is the faculty of spontaneous activity, the awareness of all our powers.

He continued with the perceptive point that if life has been filled with play 'memory will find it empty'. Thus it seems that for us humans 'time can only be *filled* by action'.

A vocational person is one who shows creativeness within certain kinds of role. If he or she has found their vocation they are not only in the part that best 'fits' them but they are bringing to it their essential and individual qualities. The requirements of the role are fulfilled – as with an actor who knows her lines and delivers them on cue – but if she is truly creative the role she is playing and the person she is are fused into one. Similarly, if you are vocational, you don't teach for a living – you *are* a teacher. As the Christian author and playwright Dorothy L. Sayers affirms:

> Work is the natural exercise and function of man . . . Work is not primarily a thing one does to live, but the thing one lives to do. It is, or should be, the full expression of the

worker's faculties, the thing in which he finds spiritual, mental and bodily satisfaction, and the medium in which he offers himself to God.

5. Enthusiasm

'Nothing great in this world was achieved without enthusiasm,' said Emerson. An extreme liking for something, especially for an activity which you undertake with gusto, verve and exuberance, is what we mean by *enthusiasm*. To love your work – or, if you prefer it, to hold an extremely favourable judgement of it, one that contains few reservations – is close to the heart of it. Enthusiasm is a great, if often overlooked, gift. Cherish it in yourself and in others.

Enthusiasm derives from a Greek word meaning to be inspired; it comes in turn from *en* (in) and *theos* (god). For the Greeks an inspired or enthusiastic person was one temporarily possessed by a god or a divine spirit, hence the strong excitement of feeling. It therefore also has a conceptual link with the idea of vocation being something given as if from outside us.

Nowadays *passion* is often used as a synonym for enthusiasm. It is actually a much stronger word suggesting something that stirs deep within and is sometimes ungovernable. Enthusiasm, by contrast, is broader in scope. It encompasses, for example, a lively or eager interest in something or someone, or a burning admiration for a cause or activity, or for a wide mixture of all of these things.

A born enthusiast may not always turn out to be a vocational person, but the importance of enthusiasm is that it is a sustainable rocket fuel for vocation. It compels action. It sends you into your natural orbit and sustains you effortlessly there. It is actually difficult to be very effective without this enthusiasm for what you are doing. Certainly, without it, excellence in performance will elude you.

It is the calling of teacher, parent and leader to locate and ignite this fuel of enthusiasm. My favourite definition of a true teacher is 'one whose actual lesson may be forgotten, but whose living enthusiasm is a quickening, animating and inspiring power'.

As Robert Browning said, 'It's no good trying to shine if you don't take time to fill your lamp'. Even enthusiasts need to avoid burn-up, but generally with such people there's plenty of fuel left in the tanks, whatever the gauge reads. They seem connected with subterranean springs of it.

Enthusiasm is linked also to energy or vitality. People with a real zest for their work – dynamic vigour along with uninhibited enjoyment – often have the kind of physical energy that keeps them going when others are flagging or when they have had little sleep.

6. Humility

'The work itself, of which he is the servant, will keep him humble; and indeed complete absence of vanity and self-importance may be the truest signs of genuine vocation.' So wrote Dorothy Emmet in her days as a philosophy professor at Manchester University. Not all vocational people are totally free of arrogance, vanity, conceit, presumption or self-assertiveness, but the greatest among them are.

Modesty is an understated acceptance of one's abilities in relation to those of others. From the Latin *modus*, a limit, modesty implies staying within boundaries and an inbred wish to avoid any form of boasting. 'I have no special gift; I am only passionately curious,' said Albert Einstein. 'I am not a great painter,' wrote Claude Monet to a friend. Excellence always eludes us, though we occasionally touch its hem. 'Have you any remaining ambitions?' Graham Greene was asked at the age of eighty. 'Yes,' replied the novelist. 'I should like to write a very good book.' That is humility.

Humility comes from the Latin *humus*, ground or earth. It suggests lowliness or smallness. But the best modern definition is a negative one: a humble person lacks arrogance.

Humility – A Test of Greatness

I believe the first test of a truly great man is his humility. I do not mean by humility doubt of his own power, or hesitation in speaking his opinions; but a right understanding of the relation between, what *he* can do and say, and the rest of the world's sayings and doings. All great men not only know their business, but usually know that they know it, and are not only right in their main opinions, but they usually know that they are right in them; only, they do not think much of themselves on that account.

Arnolfo knows he can build a good dome at Florence; Albrecht Dürer writes clearly to one who had found fault in his work, 'It could not have been done better'; Sir Isaac Newton knows that he has worked out a problem or two that would have puzzled anybody else; – only they do not expect their fellow men therefore to fall down and worship them; they have a curious under-sense of powerlessness, feeling that the greatness is not *in* them, but *through* them; that they could not do or be anything else than God made them. And they see something Divine and God-made in every other man they meet, and are endlessly, foolishly, incredibly merciful.

John Ruskin, *Modern Painters* (1843)

Being free of arrogance, vocational people are always willing to learn. Therefore they tend to become better than others in their work. Real excellence and humility are not incompatible one with the other. *On the contrary they are like natural twins.*

7. Tenacity

Walter Gropius, the late world-famous architect, wrote to a student who had asked for career advice:

'For whatever profession, your inner devotion to the tasks you have set yourself must be so deep that you can never be deflected from your aim. However often the thread may be torn out of your hands, you must develop enough patience to wind it up again and again.

'Act as if you were going to live forever and cast your plans way ahead. By this I mean that you must feel responsible without time limitation, and the consideration whether you may or may not be around to see the result should never enter your thoughts. If your contribution has been vital, there will always be somebody to pick up where you left off, and that will be your claim to immortality.'

Robert Reinhold, *New York Times* April 1992.

'So deep that you can never be deflected from your aim . . .' Therein lies the source of tenacity in the face of difficulties. 'My only strength lies in my tenacity,' said Louis Pasteur. That's the spirit of vocation: never give up. If the wind forsakes you, get out the oars.

Tenacity means holding firmly on to your purpose. Persistence, perseverance, unwillingness to admit defeat, stubbornness in adversity – all are variations on the same theme. Sticking to your aim, however, doesn't imply that kind of mindless consistency which Emerson once called 'the hobgoblin of little minds'. You can be tenacious about ends while being completely flexible about means.

Tenacity is not, thank heavens, the same as strength of character. Tenacity is a form of strength which even weak people can show, and thereby grow stronger. It is the spirit that can go on in spite of failure and keep trying again. Tomorrow is always another day.

'There are but two roads that lead to an important goal and to the doing of great things – strength and perseverance,' wrote

Goethe. 'Strength is the lot of a few privileged men; but austere perseverance, steady and continuous, may be employed by the smallest of us and rarely fails of its purpose, *for its silent power grows irresistibly greater with time.*'

8. Service

'We cannot live only for ourselves,' wrote Herman Melville. 'A thousand fibres connect us with our fellow men; and among these fibres, as sympathetic threads, our actions run as causes, and they come back to us as effects.'

The Roman word *servus*, a slave, is the origin of our English word service. It may be not too fanciful to suggest that some of the negative overtones of *servitium*, slavery, still cling to our concept of service. Like the citizens of ancient Rome many of us would prefer to be served by others – and to have the money to pay for their services – rather than to serve.

Yet it was a Roman emperor – the philosopher Marcus Aurelius – who said, 'Men exist for mutual service.' A service is an act that one person performs for another. The content or nature of a service varies, but it is always a contribution to the other person's welfare or benefit. It meets one or more of our human and individual needs. Any act of helping or benefitting another, any instance of beneficial, useful or friendly action, may count as service.

Vocational people sometimes talk about serving their work, as if the task they have accepted is a master which makes imperious demands. Dorothy L. Sayers, for example, was insistent that an artist serves first and foremost the needs of the creative work, and only secondarily and indirectly serves other people. Those in less creative fields, however, may have a much more direct sense of making a contribution to people. That sense tends to be present in seed and grow stronger with the passage of time in vocational people. They are orientated more to serving than to being served. Indeed it is a central tenet in their personal religion or philosophy, regardless of creed or culture. 'There is no higher religion than human service,' wrote Albert Schweitzer, 'To work for the common good is the greatest creed.'

9. Love

> *To business that we love we rise betime*
> *And go to with delight.*
>
> William Shakespeare

Vocational people tend to use the word 'love' in relation to their work, but even if they do not they certainly show signs of it. Vocational people are greatly attached to their work; they do not retire unless they are forced to do so by ill-health or some other compelling circumstance. The comedian Eric Morecambe, for example, had his last heart attack and died on stage, after the curtains had closed on his act. So did his fellow comedian Tommy Cooper. Peter Ustinov was once asked when he wished to die. 'At the end of a sentence', he replied.

'*No man will find the best way to do a thing unless he loves to do that thing,*' says the Japanese proverb. Wherever you find someone doing something superbly well you will also, if you probe deeply, discover that they in fact love the work they do.

Vocational work is always the best means a person can find who seeks to give, to give generously to others. An artist does this by sharing their gifts, but the difference between you or me and a great artist is one of degree not kind.

'To me every person is an artist,' writes the singer Dame Janet Baker. 'Every person has the sacred duty to pass on to others his unique experience of the world. It is the responsibility of each individual to seek the inner self and give back unstintingly and wholeheartedly whatever he finds within. It is in this sharing that individuality remains sane, and it is in the damming up of our unique natures and the desire to keep what we are for ourselves that danger lies. Anyone who deliber-

A Clear Stream – Winifred Holtby

'My existence seems to me like a clear stream which has simply reflected other people's stories and problems,' wrote Winifred Holtby, the Yorkshire novelist in a letter declining a request to write her autobiography. When she died at the early age of 37, she was mourned all over the world. For besides her novels – her final and best novel *South Riding* (1936) has been continuously in print ever since – Holtby was a fearless social reformer and campaigner for minorities. Her most passionate commitment was to the idea of service, and she pursued her mission of service to humankind with a single-mindedness that sometimes dismayed family and friends who wanted a more exclusive relationship. When one friend complained to her about her frantic life and her tendency to promote 'causes in front of friendship' Winifred replied with honesty: 'Love me if you can. If not, don't be grieved. Just give me up as one of those who went their own way in the belief that – for them – it was the only way possible.'

In South Africa her involvement with the black Industrial and Commercial Workers' Union, a cause to which she gave considerable sums of money and wrote literally millions of words in support, appeared to be fruitless. But, as she said, 'better to be the willing scribe of one permanent movement for releasing the human spirit, than produce nothing but ephemeral fiction'.

Her South African Memorial in Johannesburg is the Winifred Holtby Memorial Library.

In the quiet countryside churchyard of Rudstone, near Bridlington, her gravestone carries this inscription:

> *God give me work*
> *Till my life shall end,*
> *And life*
> *Till my work is done.*

ately refuses to give what he is and what he has back to the world diminishes the human race. There is nothing more fulfilling than the outpouring of the individual nature in any sphere. Let us rejoice in our individuality, but let us be very sure we develop it for the benefit of others. Let us share our thoughts, our inspirations, our joys and sorrows. Let us communicate.'

If love is to do with a generous giving of oneself, a willingness to share all that you have and are, then vocational people sometimes show us love in action. As the French proverb says, '*He gives nothing who does not give himself*'.

The obligation to love has no end, so neither do the demands of vocation. In his written reflections Dag Hammarskjöld reminded himself: 'You have not done enough, you have never done enough so long as it is still possible that you have something to contribute.'

At this point it might be worth looking again at the list of vocational characteristics which, if you completed the exercise at the beginning of this chapter, you may have beside you. Think again about the people you identified – both those known to you personally and the others you have read about or seen on television. Can you see more in them now? Are there other attributes or values – ones I have not mentioned – which stand out?

You should find that doing the exercise and reading this chapter has made you more aware of the much-neglected vocational dimension in work. You can put the hypothesis to the test by keeping a notebook at hand and noting any examples of vocation you come across in the next weeks, either in your daily life or books or in the media. Vocational people are not rare birds; they are as common as sparrows if you know where to look. So this is not a difficult assignment!

Don't worry if you fall a long way short: the fact that you have read this far shows that you are interested enough to persevere until you have found your vocation.

CHECKLIST – Are You a Vocational Person Yet?

Do you feel a long-term commitment to your present occupation or field of work?

Has anyone used the adjective *dedicated* to describe you or the way you go about your work?

Do you feel that your abilities match the requirements of your particular role or function?

Can you think of another profession, trade or field that you would rather be in?

Does your present work give you scope for creativity?

Are you adventurous by nature, always seeking new and better ways of doing things?

Have you discovered work that you can be really enthusiastic about, in spite of its ups and downs?

Has your enthusiasm for your work been tested and sustained over a period of years?

Do you have a sense of being, as it were, at the call of your work, and through your work to others?

Is humility – the opposite of arrogance – a characteristic of the way you talk about your work and conduct yourself in it?

In face of difficulties have you shown a power to endure them and to overcome obstacles?

Faced with monotonous failures are you always willing to give it another go?

Summary of Key Points

- Vocation is hard to define but easy to see when it is present in the lives of others. Vocational people share some common characteristics, such as (1) dedication, (2)'fit' between their abilities and the calls of their work, (3) a lack of mercenary spirit, (4) personal creativity, (5) enthusiasm or passion, (6) humility and (7) tenacity, in the face of difficulties, (8) a sense of service and (9) love of their work.
- Dedication or commitment is the most obvious or clearly observable quality that vocational people share. It is linked to a lifelong enthusiasm for what you do.
- Vocation tends to be long-term if not lifelong, and it is not necessarily linked to paid employment.
- 'To create is always to do something new,' said Martin Luther. Vocation is directly or indirectly connected with creativity. Even in traditional occupations or well-established fields vocational people seek new ways of doing things. They are society's agents of change – the change for good we call progress.
- Vocational people tend to be – or become – strong characters. Yet, paradoxically, they are the most unselfconscious of all people. Despite their gifts or attainments they have a sense of their relative smallness in the great unfolding pattern of life.
- Perseverance is essential. Don't give up too easily. As an oriental proverb says, 'There is marrow in this bone if you will but probe it.'
- Besides creativity the other star in the vocational sky is service. 'I am never weary of being useful,' wrote Leonardo da Vinci. 'In serving others I cannot do enough – no labour is sufficient to tire me.' But you don't have to be a Leonardo to make service of others your end: it is an optional way of interpreting every job, trade or profession. 'No one is useless in this world who lightens the burdens of another,' said Charles Dickens.

- The Bedouin say that 'What comes from your heart is greater than what comes from the hand only.' To have found your vocation means that your heart and soul are in your work, not just brain or hand. Work can now become a means of practical love – love in action.

> *Does the road wind uphill all the way?*
> *Yes, to the very end.*
> *Will the day's journey take the whole long day?*
> *From morn to night, my friend.*
>
> Christina Rossetti

2

The 'Myth' of Vocation

Every person has their vocation. The talent is the call.

Ralph Waldo Emerson

By myth I don't mean something that is untrue, but a timeless story which provides a series of answers to age-old questions asked in every generation: Why do some do better than others? What should you do with your life? How shall we be judged? What is success?

The Parable of the Talents is a familiar story in the Christian Gospels, but I believe that it has a universal application. For me, it embodies the essential nature – the myth – of vocation.

What this parable may or may not have meant to those who heard Jesus tell it need not detain us here. Parables are like poems, enigmatic messages in metaphorical nutshells. A picture, poem or parable may carry truths other than what its creator has in mind or what its first audience – with their particular concerns and interests – read into it. That is the essence of art. What truth does it carry to us about the nature of vocation?

There are in fact two versions of the Parable of the Talents (Matthew 25: 14–30 and Luke 19: 11–27). Here is Matthew's version:

For it will be as when a man going on a journey called his servants and entrusted to them his property; to one he gave five talents, to another two, to another one, to each according to his ability. Then he went away.

He who had received the five talents went at once and traded with them; and he made five talents more. So also, he who had the two talents made two talents more. But he who had received the one talent went out and dug in the ground and hid his master's money.

Now after a long time the master of those servants came and settled accounts with them. And he who had received the five talents came forward, bringing five talents more, saying, 'Master, you delivered to me five talents; here I have made five talents more.' His master said to him, 'Well done, good and faithful servant; you have been faithful over a little, I will set you over much; enter into the joy of your master.'

And he also who had the two talents came forward, saying, 'Master, you delivered to me two talents; here I have made two talents more.' His master said to him, 'Well done, good and faithful servant; you have been faithful over a little, I will set you over much; enter into the joy of your master.'

He also who had received one talent came forward, saying, 'Master, I knew you to be a hard man, reaping where you did not sow, and gathering where you did not winnow; so I was afraid, and I went out and hid your talent in the ground. Here you have what is yours.'

But his master answered him, 'You wicked and slothful servant! You knew that I reap where I have not sowed, and gather where I have not winnowed? Then you ought to have invested my money with the bankers, and at my coming I should have received what was my own with interest. So take the talent from him, and give it to him who has the ten talents. For to everyone who has will more be given, and he will have abundance; but from him who has not, even what he has will be taken away. And cast the worthless servant into the outer darkness; there men will weep and gnash their teeth.'

What is Our Talent?

The Parable of the Talents is directly relevant to us because it gives us that key word – *talent*. For us, a talent means a natural aptitude, but that was not the original meaning of the word, as doubtless you will have guessed. We have read *our* meaning into the word by a process of creative interpretation.

A talent was originally a large lump of precious metal used in the ancient world as a medium of exchange. Our word comes from the Latin – *talentum*, which in turn derives from the Greek *talantum*, either a balance for weighing money or

---

The Spectrum of Natural Abilities

GENIUS   A mental power beyond explanation in terms of heritage or education, which manifests itself by exceptional originality and extraordinary intelligence, surpassing that of most superior people. *Example*: Leonardo da Vinci. May be applied particularly to one area. *Example*: Mozart

GIFT   *Gift* is akin to *genius* but on a lower plane. It suggests a great natural ability, emphasizing inborn quality. Literally it means 'something given' and often implies a special favour by God or nature. It may apply to any striking or remarkable personal ability or power.

TALENT   A particular, uncommon aptitude for some special work or activity; it is conceived of as an inborn resource that may or may not be developed. Whereas *genius* usually applies to general intellectual or artistic superiority, *talent* is a specific natural endowment or gift. It can stand also for the sum of the natural endowment of a person.

ABILITY	The quality or state of being able (from Latin *habilis*, apt, skilful). *Ability* is stronger than *aptitude* in implying competence in doing or skill.
SKILL	*Skill*, from an Old Norse word, is roughly synonymous with *ability* – the ability to use one's knowledge effectively in execution or performance, technical expertise. A *skill* is a learned power of doing a thing competently. It is a *developed* aptitude or ability. It may refer, most simply, to relatively commonplace abilities gained largely through training. But it may also refer to ability that training alone could not account for without considerable natural talent, such as the skill of a prima ballerina.
APTITUDE	A natural or acquired ability to learn and become proficient; a natural liking for some activity and the likelihood of success in it. It suggests quickness in learning. It derives from the Latin *aptus*, literally meaning 'fastened' – usually fitted, qualified or suited to its purpose.

the weight itself. The value of a talent varied. In coined money in Greece it was equal to 6000 drachmas or in Palestine to 3000 shekels. In weight in both Athens and Rome the talent was about 60 *minas* (nearly 57 lbs or 26 kilograms). There were talents of gold and copper, but silver was the most common currency. Clearly a talent of silver was a very substantial sum of money.

The original high monetary value of *talent* is reflected in our modern usage of it in the context of natural abilities or aptitudes, as the table shows. There is a spectrum of words in

English for innate or natural ability, ranging from what is extremely rare through the unusual to the more common. Talent comes quite high up the scale.

As you will see, not surprisingly there are considerable overlaps between these words. But we do have some sort of valuing hierarchy when it comes to describing natural or acquired personal abilities. Talent comes quite far up the list; it is uncommon but not rare. But notice, too, its more general if less frequent use to describe the sum of a person's natural endowments. In that sense *you* are your talent.

It is important to remind ourselves that we *all* have abilities at some of these levels. Moreover, we should guard against confusing *aptitudes* – something you are naturally (very) good at – with *skills*, your set of proficiencies as developed by training. All of us have a lot more raw potential in us in the form of aptitudes than we manage to convert into specific skills.

Why Do Talented People Tend To Work Harder?

One of the principal psychological truths about vocation which the story reflects in a mythic way is a simple principle: *a great aptitude is matched by great motivation, a small aptitude by small motivation.* Mozart needed no outside stimulus to apply himself to music. Yet a child with little or no musical aptitude has to be driven to the piano to practise.

The servants who received five and two talents were much more productive than the servant who only received one. The story hints that the latter's problem was in part motivational – the Master, you recall, calls him 'slothful'. Sloth means a marked disinclination to work or take trouble, coupled with a temperamental inability to act promptly or speedily when action or speed is called for. Now sloth or lethargy can indeed be a *temperamental* tendency but those with greater talents or gifts seem to overcome it much better than those with only small aptitudes. It is natural to like work that you have ability for, and the more ability you have the more you like it and want to do it.

Highly talented people, then, tend to be highly motivated. It is as if the gift in them demands to be served, used and multiplied. The Parable reflects this phenomenon accurately. In writing about his own vocation John Bunyan said: 'But yet I could not be content, unless I was found in the exercise of my gift, *unto which also I was greatly animated.*' That animation – the presence of motion or activity in what otherwise might be torpid if not lifeless – is almost invariably found in the really gifted.

A Task-Shaped Need in Our Lives?

In the parable, the demanding or exacting nature of vocational work is personified in the Absent Master. It is he who imposes the general task of vocation – use your talents to the full – upon humankind. Some of the servants respond better to this than others. This illustrates another essential aspect of the myth of vocation.

Our word *task* derives from the old Norman-French *tasque*, a tax or service imposed by a feudal superior. A task is usually an assigned piece of work, often to be finished within a certain time. Sometimes it carries overtones of something hard or unpleasant, but it is always something *that has to be done*. There is too, a sense about a task that it is *imposed* upon you by an employer or teacher, or by circumstance. You don't have all that much choice – if any – in the matter, just as you are not at liberty to decide whether or not to pay your income tax this year.

It is not surprising that we sometimes try to escape from the tasks that arise before us. But vocation moves in the opposite direction. It means being ready and willing to be given tasks to do, however demanding. When Isaiah saw his vision in the Temple at Jerusalem of God enthroned in splendour like an oriental King, conferring in council, 'I heard the voice of the Lord saying, "Whom shall I send, and who will go for us?"

Then I said, "Here I am! Send me." And he said, "Go, and say to this people . . ."'

What this suggests to me is that we are *made* for tasks. If we do not discover real and challenging tasks to do we invent them in the form of sport, exploration or war. The natural elements, for example, become a taskmaster to the sailor, mountaineer or pilot.

In 1993 a paper was read at the British Psychological Society by John Haworth (of the Department of Psychology at the University of Manchester) which confirmed what vocational people know already, namely that work is more satisfying than leisure. This isn't because paid employment brings self-esteem as well as money, but *because it forces you to do things you would rather avoid.* Sounds like the Absent Master in the parable!

The journalist Libby Purves commented on this research finding in *The Times* (27 September), and added some personal experiences as support:

> I could have told them that. There is nothing like a stern taskmaster to enhance anybody's life from the age of four upwards.
>
> Happy is the pupil whose teacher makes her finish the page, and whose university tutor actually expects the essay on time. In your first job, the best thing a fairy godmother could offer is a guarantee that someone in charge will care enough to make you do sloppy work over again. The best teachers and bosses achieve a kind of immortality: years later, their inexorable voices ring in your head and make you do things properly. Which leads, in the end, to happiness.
>
> The first time I consciously experienced this effect was at Oxford, under the immensely aged doyen of Anglo-Saxon grammar, Professor C. L. Wrenn. It was not much fun: even half-blind and hobbling, he had a sarcastic, critical tongue which would strip paint. When he died in mid-term, of pure old age, our first reaction was, shamingly, 'Phew! We won't have to finish that translation!'

Our second instinct was to finish it, in his memory and honour. And we did.

Libby Purves applied the same principle to mothers 'who get the same clandestine thrill from the remorselessness of their children's demands'. You have no desire to get up at 3 a.m. to tend to a sick child 'but you have no choice'. Women without jobs who collapse in depression when their children leave home, she suggested, may be suffering from taskmaster-deprivation! Tasks give us a clear sense of purpose and the more demanding they are, the greater the satisfaction we may derive from knowing that they are ours to fulfil.

For religious people it would be natural to equate the Absent Master in the parable with God the creator, who walked in the cool of the evening with Adam in the Garden of Eden in the opening chapters of Genesis. God, of course, is *like* the Absent Master in that he cannot be perceived with our senses, but *unlike* him in that he is always present.

To live in – or as if in – the *presence* of one's divine Taskmaster is the challenge of those with a vocation to religious faith. Yet that is what a vocation to God's service requires. In a sonnet entitled 'On being arrived to the age of 23' the great Christian poet, John Milton expressed his self-dedication to live and work daily 'as ever in my great Taskmaster's eye'.

With the relative eclipse of God in our time, it might be thought that the influence of this concept of a 'great Taskmaster' would also have waned. But we still feel the gravitational pull in the form of a sense of obligation or duty. Indian culture, for example, arguably one of the most spiritually aware on earth, is dominated by the concept of duty – one of the refracted beams from the great Taskmaster's eye.

Duty, from another old French word, *deu*, is the conduct due to parents or superiors, the action required by your position or occupation, the sum of your moral or legal obligations. It is a universal concept. What is the relation of duty to vocation? William Wordsworth captures it in his *Ode to Duty*:

Stern Daughter of the Voice of God!
O Duty! If that name thou love
Who art a light to guide, a rod
To check the erring, and reprove . . .

Duty is like a *daughter* – one remove away – of vocation. Unlike obligation it is a more internal awareness. It tells us what we *ought* to do. Like the reflected light from the moon, it seems a cold concept, but it is better than nothing in the still of the night and it will serve to point us in the right direction.

The Task of Mozart

Mozart was only thirty-five when he died in 1791 and was buried in a pauper's grave. His short life was beset by personal problems and financial worries. His faithless wife betrayed him. The citizens of his native Salzburg were unresponsive – 'When I play, or when any of my compositions are performed, it is just as if the audience were all tables and chairs.' His employer, the Archbishop of Salzburg, dismissed him. Yet central to Mozart's life was his sense of vocation. He never lost his sense of his divinely appointed task. 'I am a composer and was born to be a Kapellmeister. I neither can nor ought to bury the talent for composition with which God in his goodness has so richly endowed me.'

The tasks that come to us or parade for our acceptance are often hard, severe or even apparently impossible. The inner feeling is that this thing has to be done, in spite of its cost in labour or difficulty, the trials it may bring or the burden it imposes. A great task is one that makes great demands on your abilities and resources. The enjoyment is more in retrospect. As the inventor Barnes Wallis once said, 'There is nothing so enjoyable in life than being told a thing is impossible and then proving that it can be done.'

A Gift that Alters the Picture?

So far I have interpreted the Parable of Talents as a natural story with mythic proportions. There is actually nothing specifically religious about it (some, as I have said, may well *assume* that the Master is a figure for God but we are not *told* that). As I have outlined, I believe the story reflects several truths about the natural phenomenon of highly talented and less-talented people and how we experience a task-shaped gap in our lives. Vocation fills that void. It is not that divine tasks come to us on a celestial internet, but that the mixture of purpose, values, situational needs and creative energy always throws up new and worthwhile challenges.

From the embers of yesterday's tasks arise, phoenix-like, challenges that come to us today and will do so tomorrow. They are irresistible magnets in every sphere of human activity, and the harder they are the better. As John Hunt, leader of the 1953 Everest Expedition wrote after the first conquest of the world's highest mountain: 'There is no height, no depths, that the spirit of man guided by a higher spirit cannot attain.'

Grace is what makes the difference. It means literally a gift, from the Latin *gratia*. It can be contrasted with nature, although in fact there is more a continuum between the two. For example, we talk about extremely rare talents as gifts or graces, as if they are somehow inexplicable as simply natural phenomena. Whether this is fact or feeling I must leave to you to judge, but what matters is that we do distinguish what seems to come to us as a gift.

Seamus Heaney, Nobel Prize-winner for his poetry, says that he does not like being described as a professional poet, because he fears that the definition deprives writing of its sense of advent. 'For three years after I left Belfast and went to live in Wicklow, I was a full-time writer,' he recalls. 'I regard that period as crucial to my confirmation as poet. It was like a

sacrament and it gave me a sense of being that nothing else
has given me in my life. But I would say teaching is my profession. Poetry is a grace.'

Grace is like a salt that flavours natural vocation and brings
out its true taste. *God does not destroy nature but perfects it.*
This, the great insight of St Thomas Aquinas, invites us to
explore how grace does work to transform our natural concept
of vocation as reflected in the mirror of the myth. It is as if an
artist takes nature and subtly draws out a deeper meaning.

The first artist to do so as far as the Parable of the Talents
was concerned was Luke, who sets the story more firmly in
the realm of grace. The Master, for example, is altered into a
Lord who goes into a far country to receive a kingdom – a
hint for Christians as to his true identity.

Before his departure the Lord calls *ten* of his servants and
gives each of them the *same* amount of silver – a pound in
some English translations. He tells them, 'Trade with these
until I come.' On his return three servants come before him.
One has turned his pound into ten; another into five; while
the third reported he had hid his one in a napkin 'for I was
afraid of you, because you are a severe man'.

By extending the number of servants and by lowering the
value of the 'talent' to a mere pound – one-sixtieth of a real
talent – Luke is inviting all his readers to see themselves in the
story. The natural reflection – that those with great talent are
greatly motivated – is not subtly altered. All aptitudes, whatever their natural size, are spiritually the same in value in the
eyes of the Lord. *It is not the size of your aptitude that matters,
it is what you do with it.*

To make much out of little suggests the presence of grace;
it is contrary to what we expect from nature. John Bunyan
summed it up: 'Great grace and small gifts are better than great
gifts and no grace.'

It is not as if grace works like some celestial tiger in your
fuel tank. On that Thomist principle *grace does not destroy
nature but perfects it* the function of this gift we call grace is
to work upon and transform natural vocation so that it is, if

anything, more natural, more fully itself, more *you* – the best you.

Exercise

Imagine that the Master in the parable leaves at home a beautiful daughter. For some reason she falls in love with the young and handsome servant who has slothfully buried the talent given him, intent upon the pleasures of the moment. He falls passionately in love with her, too, and wants nothing else in the world but to marry her. 'You know what my father is like,' she warns, with a sigh. What will the young man do? Now rewrite the story.

What Is Success in Vocation?

The Parable of the Talents is a story about true success and failure in life. To succeed is to use all the talent that is given you as fully as you can in the changing circumstances in which you find yourself. Conversely, to fail is to bury your talent; it is to hide the lighted candle of your life under a cover, so that the lack of oxygen eventually causes the flame to flicker, fade and die.

As Thomas Wolfe wrote in *You Can't Go Home Again* (1940):

> If a man has talent and cannot use it, he has failed. If he has a talent and uses only half of it, he has partly failed. If he has talent and learns somehow to use the whole of it, he has gloriously succeeded, and won a satisfaction and a triumph few men ever know.

In the story the concept of true success or failure in life is taught by the *consequences* of pursuing each of the two courses of action. Again, the story is remarkably accurate in what tends to happen. If you fail, or 'bury your talent', it atrophies. It decreases in size and begins to waste away, like an immobilized limb or muscle. As the modern proverb warns: *Use it or lose it.*

As for what the world calls success – titles, status, wealth, possessions, fame – vocational people seldom court it directly. 'I dread success,' said George Bernard Shaw, while Robert Louis Stevenson suggested that the right course is 'to continue to fail in good spirits'. Anthony Trollope regarded success as 'the necessary misfortune of life, but it is only to the very unfortunate that it comes early'. Perhaps part of this suspicion stems from the fact that success so often breeds later failure, that the character grows more in adversity than in prosperity.

Conversely true success – the full employment of all that has been, as it were, entrusted to you – attracts the opposite consequences. *More* resources are given to the 'profitable' servants, namely the talent left idle by their dismissed colleague. *More* opportunity now comes their way. They are 'set over much' or, in Luke's version, over ten and five cities respectively. There is a third reward, too, which is 'to enter into the joy' of the Master.

Again all this ties in well with what we know about vocational people. Their abilities multiply, both in range and quality. They have more choices as they progress: more challenging and professionally interesting opportunities come their way. And enjoyment, as we have seen, is a hallmark of vocational people. They are paid in the coinage of joy.

At one level, then, the myth reflects what is universally true. The Master in Luke's version sums up the message succinctly: *To everyone who has more will be given; but from him who has not, even what he has will be taken away.*

How does grace alter that natural picture? A widow with two copper farthings to her name, who casts them generously into the treasury for the relief of suffering, has given of her substance. That is the measure of success in the Kingdom of God. Grace is always paradoxical. It is the gift of strength to those afflicted by weakness. It is the gift of dedication and enthusiasm to those with little to offer. So it can transform

The Weight of Glory

'Once philosopher-psychologist Henri Bergson asked Pablo Casals what he felt when he was playing the music of Bach or Beethoven. Casals replied that if he was satisfied with his performance, he had an almost physical sensation of bearing a tangible weight of something inestimably precious within. He likened it to carrying inside himself a lump of gold.'

H. L. Kirk, *Pablo Casals: A Biography*

There are few commoner words in the English Bible than 'glory' and few more difficult to define. Reputation, praise, honour (true and false), splendour, light, perfection, rewards (temporal and eternal) – all these various conceptions seem covered by the same word.

Nevertheless the underlying thought is simpler than it would appear. In the most common Hebrew word translated by 'glory' the root idea is 'heaviness' or 'weight', and so in a metaphorical sense 'worthiness'. As the early Hebrews had not the use of coined money, which was of a certain determined weight, they weighed all gold and silver they used in trade. And so that 'lump of gold' which Casals felt inside him after an excellent performance may have been a measure of 'an eternal weight of glory', as St Paul calls it (2 Corinthians 4:17).

even the humblest calling. As Oliver Wendell Holmes once said, 'Every calling is great when greatly pursued.'

Summary of Key Points

- Sometimes a simple story tells us more than volumes of academic discourse. The Parable of the Talents – from whence comes our key word *talent* – is more than an enigmatic comparison or a metaphor. It may serve us as a myth, reflecting some natural truths about vocation and also answering the implied question: 'What should we do with our lives?'

- Great abilities are usually paired with a strong and persistent inner impulse to use them. Conversely, small measures of aptitude are accompanied by weaker natural motivation.
- Never bury a talent. A Chinese proverb teaches: *A wise man does not lay up treasure. The more he gives, the more he has.*
- 'Rewards' and 'penalties' is quasi-legal language. But there are natural consequences, either for good or ill, which come to those who employ their talents and to those who neglect them. These consequences are not expressions of the arbitrary will of a 'stern Master'. The myth reflects the way things are. More comes to those who use their talents; those who don't run the risk of losing the faculty itself through disuse.
- 'You would not think any duty small if you were great,' said George Macdonald. Luke suggests that our 'talents' or 'pounds' are all of the *same* spiritual value, whatever their natural rarity. What differentiates us is how we use or misuse our talent. That is not literally (or naturally) true: Michelangelo, Mozart and Einstein cannot be compared to you or me. But, in *vocational* terms, their success is not greater than that of someone who uses their much more modest talent to the full in their occupations.
- 'Our chief want in life is somebody who will make us do what we can,' says Emerson. Taskmasters – external people or circumstances – are the rockets under us which propel us into the effortless orbit of vocation, where work is fun.
- Grace may be contrasted to Nature, but its principal function is to complete or perfect what is natural to us.

There is a place and means for every one alive.
William Shakespeare, *All's Well That Ends Well*

3

The Way Ahead

There's a divinity that shapes our ends,
Rough-hew them how we will.

William Shakespeare

In the Preface I suggested that the best way to find your vocation is to fulfil the necessary conditions in the confidence that if you do so then the *other* – some power beyond ourselves or, if you prefer, the Unknown God – will complete the process by supplying the sufficient condition that ensures that you are on your true course in life. One of those necessary conditions is *a working knowledge of your own talents*, and that is the subject of the following chapter. Here I shall discuss two other necessary conditions: *having a clear vocational aim* and *committing yourself to it*. And then I shall conclude by giving some examples of what might be called the sufficient condition at work – the deep mysterious 'Yes' of vocation.

A Clear Vocational Aim

In Shakespeare's plays *Henry VI* Parts 1 and 2 and *The Merry Wives of Windsor*, Sir John Falstaff is portrayed as the boon companion of Henry, Prince of Wales. He is a fat, sensual, unscrupulous, boastful and mendacious knight, full of wit and humour. Dr Samuel Johnson once called him 'unimitated, unimitable' and 'a compound of sense and vice'. A lover of wine and jests, Falstaff is an old rogue with a twinkle in his eye: he can use his quick wit to turn a joke against him to his own advantage. Here he is in action:

Prince. I see a good amendment of life in thee: from praying
to purse-taking.

Falstaff. Why, Hal, 'tis vocation, Hal; 'tis no sin for a man to
labour in his vocation.

On the surface Falstaff sounds plausible. His natural abilities
are arguably being fully employed in stealing purses; it is his
chosen occupation. Why not call it a vocation? In fact we know
intuitively – and probably Falstaff knows as well – that being
a cat-burglar, mugger, thief or bank-robber is not a vocation.
But why not?

The answer in a nutshell is that purse-taking or mugging
does not contribute either to the good of the particular individual on the receiving end, or to society as a whole. In fact
it does positive harm to both.

In the case of Shakespeare's Falstaff we know what is happening. Hypocrisy, it has been said, is the compliment that
vice pays to virtue. Falstaff (or Shakespeare) is humorously
reflecting a tendency to extend the Protestant doctrine of
vocation well beyond its intended limits. That doctrine made
love of one's neighbour by direct, first-hand action, using one's
talents or skills, the end of all work. Hence it invited all ranks
and orders of Christian society, including merchants, trades-
men, craftsman and labourers, to perceive the dignity of divine
vocation in their daily work. As Martin Luther said, 'A dairy-
maid can milk cows to the glory of God.'

The Protestant reformers of the sixteenth century, of course,
lived in a world of villages, towns and cities, small by today's
standards, where everyone knew everyone else. In this context
work as a direct means of loving one's neighbour made sense,
for the customer or client was usually a neighbour too. In 1532
Martin Luther could tell the townsfolk of Wittenberg in a
sermon:

To use a rough example: If you are a craftsman you will
find the Bible placed in your hands, in your hearts; it teaches
and preaches how you ought to treat your neighbour. Only

look at your tools, your needle, your thimble, your beer barrel, your articles or trade, your scales, your measures and you will find this saying written on them: 'Use me toward your neighbour as you would want him to act toward you with that which is his.'

Later ages have felt the need to broaden the more concrete and homely idea of loving one's neighbour to a more universal and comprehensive principle. The great poet of Scotland, Robert Burns, offered this working definition of what constitutes doing good to others:

Whatever mitigates the woes or increases the happiness of others, this is my criterion of goodness; and whatever injures society at large, or any individual in it, this is my measure of iniquity.

In our own time we may widen the net still further to encompass contributions to the preservation of the planet, the good of the environment, and to improving the lot of other living creatures. Moreover, to the concept of goodness – doing good – we must add the pursuit of truth and beauty, for the scientist and the artist are as vocational as doctor, teacher or conservationist. For many of us, however, a large measure of satisfaction in work still comes from that direct personal service to another individual in the guise of a customer or client. A survey of 35,000 employees in the United Kingdom (*The Times*, 3 September 1999) revealed that the highest levels of job satisfaction were among those providing personal service, even if the pay was poor. Several factors contribute towards the degree to which a person is satisfied with their job – job satisfaction is not to be equated with vocation. But the factor of direct personal service stands out as the common denominator in those happy with their lot.

Those who render indirect personal service – service to the public as opposed to individuals face-to-face – are fully entitled to a sense of vocation (this is considered further in Chapter

Seven). Even those who are physically or mentally disabled from work as we tend to conceive it are enfranchised to see their lives in terms of vocation. As John Milton, afflicted with blindness, wrote in his most powerful sonnet, 'They also serve who only stand and wait'. It is as if those who have offered themselves, who are willing and waiting to serve if only they could, are treated as equals to those who are fully engaged. Soldiers in reserve are doing their duty as much as those in the front-line. In God's eyes all vocations are equal in value: it is we who perceive them differently.

Within the moral framework of your own culture, then, your vocational aim is *to identify your talents and use them to the full.*

This definition, I hasten to add, is only a template or pattern. Use it as a mould in which to crystallize into words your own statement of aim. What matters is that you should 'own' it.

Perhaps I should clarify here what I mean by 'aim', for I believe that it is important to be clear at the outset that there is a difference between general *purpose* in life and vocational *aim*. The first is more comprehensive. If you confuse your vocational *aim* with the *purpose* of life, you may end up as a workaholic!

Nothing is more important in life than directing it towards its true purpose. George Bernard Shaw wrote:

This is the true joy in life, the being used for a purpose recognised by yourself as a mighty one; the being thoroughly worn out before you are thrown on the scrap heap; the being a force of Nature instead of a feverish selfish little clod of ailments and grievances complaining that the world will not devote itself to making you happy.

Because the relation between *purpose* in life, vocational *aim* and more tangible *objectives* or *goals* is so central to this book it is worth exploring it further. That may lead you to seeing where you head for next once you have clarified your long-term vocational aim.

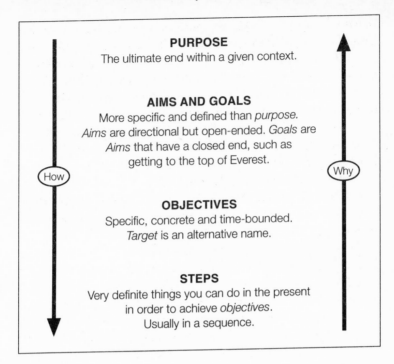

PURPOSE
The ultimate end within a given context.

AIMS AND GOALS
More specific and defined than *purpose*.
Aims are directional but open-ended. *Goals* are
Aims that have a closed end, such as
getting to the top of Everest.

How

Why

OBJECTIVES
Specific, concrete and time-bounded.
Target is an alternative name.

STEPS
Very definite things you can do in the present
in order to achieve *objectives*.
Usually in a sequence.

Figure 3.1 *Purpose, Aims, Objectives, Steps*

Purpose, Aims, Objectives and Steps

A framework for thinking about human intentions that I have found quite useful as a means of clear thinking is one that distinguishes between *purpose, aims, objectives* and *steps* and explores their relationships (see Figure 3.1). It is like that fabulous ladder in Jacob's dream in Genesis (28:12): stretching from heaven to earth, with angels descending and ascending.

You can now see that descending the Jacob's ladder, from the general and abstract to the particular and concrete, you are answering the question 'How?' This is my *purpose*. Yes, but *how* are you going to achieve it? By tackling these *aims* or *goals*.

Notice that *aims* are really no more than *purpose* broken

down into manageable parts. It is like light being refracted into the colours of the rainbow. The same is true of the next stage in the descent. Take any one *aim*. How are you going to achieve it? Answer: by achieving these *objectives*. Now pick out any of these *objectives*: how are you going to accomplish that? Answer: by taking these *steps*. Today? Yes, there's bound to be one of those *steps* that you can take right now!

Going upwards rather than downwards, you are then answering the '*why?*' question. Why are you taking this *step*? In order to achieve this *objective*. Why this *objective*? To move along that *aim* or towards that *goal*. Why that *aim/goal*? In order to fulfil my *purpose*.

Focusing on *purpose* and *aims* rather than upon one specific *goal* has three major potential benefits.

Flexibility

The most obvious advantage is greater flexibility. If you think in terms of *purpose* you can more easily alter your plans as circumstances arise. On the other hand, if you lock yourself into a goal like an intercontinental missile, then you are much more liable to be shot down and lose all. In times of change, you do have to be more general in your intention in order to give yourself maximum leeway – the allowable margin of freedom or variation. Remember that Columbus was sailing for India when he discovered America. Because his purpose was to *explore*, we do not regard him as a failure.

A Sense of Direction

A *purpose* in life, especially when refracted into more definite aims, may well develop in you a sense of overall direction. It serves like the Pole Star in the sky in that respect. You will never reach the star itself, but it can guide you to your destination.

By another analogy, your purpose should act like a magnetic force that draws you in a certain direction. You may make navigational errors, but that magnetic influence constantly affects the compass of your spirit and – if you heed it – draws you back on course. 'Our plans miscarry because they have no aim,' wrote Seneca. 'When a man does not know what harbour he is making for, no wind is the right wind.'

A Measure of Progress

From time to time, you may want to appraise yourself in terms of progress. If you think in terms of a specific objective or goal, it is relatively easy to know if you succeed or fail. I mean, either you did become President of the United States or you did not. And with goals like that there is plenty of scope for failure! As Epictetus wrote: 'One must not tie a ship to a single anchor, nor life to a single hope.'

If, on the other hand, you are focused on *purpose*, it follows that you will find it harder to experience total success or failure – only a series of successes or failures. The latter may in reality be indicators of progress, but they are imperfect measuring instruments and you will need to develop a more holistic judgement. We should seek to measure what we value, not value what we can easily measure in quantifiable ways.

Exercise

Think back to the list you made in Chapter One, of five or more people whom you consider to be truly vocational. Now choose one of them, perhaps the one you most admire or whose background is not unlike your own. Imagine that you *are* that person, young and considering your career. In one sentence write down the *purpose* or vision of your life as a whole. Now write down two or three *aims* which make that purpose a bit more concrete or tangible. Remember that aims tend to be long-term and directional. They can be either open (*aims*) or closed (*goals*).

So, that's the easy bit done! Now it gets more difficult.

What is the *vocational aim* that you should select and maintain throughout your life?

The Touchstone of Success

The test of an aim is whether or not it gives you a touchstone of success. The vocational aim that stems from the Parable of the Talents is a robust one: it will last you a lifetime. And you *can* use it as a touchstone.

A touchstone literally is a black silicous stone related to flint and formerly used to test the purity of gold and silver by the streak left on the stone when it is rubbed by the metal. As a metaphor it is a test or criterion for determining the quality or genuineness of a thing.

True Success

We shall never forget John. In his generosity of heart he was a simple and artless exemplar of what the Prayer Book calls 'loving kindness'. He used to the full the talents which his Creator had entrusted to him. He enjoyed his life fully and shared that enjoyment with countless others. At the core of his life was good humour, cheerful cordiality, playfulness, a kind of suffused gaiety of soul; Aristotle's *eutrapelia*, that gold mean between stolidity and buffoonery, that kindly affability which was very properly claimed by Thomas Aquinas as an important Christian virtue.

Obituary of John Griffith, Fellow of Jesus College, Oxford
(*Jesus College Record*)

The fullest and most effective use of your talents for the common good, incidentally, includes *your* good as well as others'. Here is the touchstone that you have to apply from time to time to what you are doing. Why not once and for all? Because, as I have already said, circumstances change and you change too. New interests arise, new skills develop, new needs emerge. 'When one door of happiness closes, another opens; but often we look so long at the closed door, that we do not see the one that has been opened for us.' The author of those words, Helen Keller, became blind, deaf and dumb at the age of nineteen months, but went on to be an author and an inspirational leader.

It is not that success in vocation is an alternative to wealth – it *is* wealth. For, as John Henry Jowett said, 'The measure of our wealth is how much we would be worth if we lost all our money.'

Crossing the Rubicon

Now we come to another crossroads – the second necessary condition. As I suggested above, a general and irrevocable commitment to that vocational aim seems to work. I cannot say that I understand how or why. Are you prepared now to commit yourself to your own version of the vocational aim – and to make it a lifelong commitment? Are you, in other words ready to wade across the Rubicon?

In 49BC, declaring '*Jacta alea esto*, Let the dice be cast!', Julius Caesar crossed the River Rubicon, the boundary between Cisalpine Gaul and Rome's own territory, thereby committing himself irrevocably to a bid for supreme power.

Casting the dice or crossing the Rubicon are metaphors for the act of decision. Remember that what you are committing yourself to is that vocation aim: in other words, to seeking to live as a vocational person for the remainder of your days. Such a Rubicon-decision is irrevocable because it will determine what you *are*. So, *look before you leap*. Or, in Caesar's language, *Caveat emptor* – 'Buyer, watch out!'

It's actually not easy to know if and when you have committed yourself in the momentous sense. You may have had the experience of committing yourself to, say, giving up smoking or going on a diet – only to find yourself accepting a cigarette or eating far too much of those foods you had shunned for ever! In *The Princess and the Goblin*, George MacDonald describes that very experience:

> He jumped up, as he thought, and began to dress, but, to his dismay, found that he was still in bed. 'Now then I will!' he said, 'Here goes! I *am* up now!' But yet again he found himself snug in bed. Twenty times he tried, and twenty times he failed: for in fact he was not awake, only dreaming that he was.

Sometimes you only know the difference between those twenty dreamy false starts and the twenty-first time, when Rubicon – the point of no return – was *really* crossed, some years later when you reflect upon your life with the benefit of hindsight. The turning point, the hinge upon which your life swung, will be clear, for your mind will always return to that time and place like a homing pigeon.

Again usually by hindsight, it looks as if that elusive *sufficient condition* has now been met. The dice you have cast on the table has been met by an answering throw. Something decisive has happened. Things will never be quite the same. You now have a sense of purpose in life. You are on the move, with a new sense of your worth and destiny as a unique person. In his book *Mount Everest Expedition* (1951), W. H. Murray wrote:

> Until one is committed there is hesitancy, the chance to draw back, always ineffectiveness. Concerning all acts of initiative (and creation), there is one elementary truth, the ignorance of which kills countless ideas and splendid plans: that the moment one definitely commits oneself, then Providence moves too. All sorts of things occur to help one that would never otherwise have occurred. A whole stream of events issues from the decision, raising in one's favour all manner of unforeseen incidents and meetings and material assistance which no man could have dreamt would have come his way. I have learned a deep respect for one of Goethe's couplets:

'Whatever you can do, or dream you can, begin it. Boldness has genius, power, and magic in it.'

'Then Providence moves too . . .' That sense that something *other* has, as it were, accepted your offer and has underwritten your enterprise invites religious language. It is not a specifically Christian experience: Socrates, for example, believed that God had called him to be a philosopher. It is as if the sufficient condition has been fulfilled. Whatever name we give it – Zeus or God, Power of Being – it is on your side. There is sometimes also a sense of assurance, even if the way ahead is clouded in doubt or beset with difficulties. It breeds an inner confidence.

The Case of the Swedish Diplomat

Born in 1905, son of a Swedish prime minister, Dag Hammarskjöld reached the pinnacle of the world civil service as Secretary General to the United Nations (1953–8). He had to deal with the Suez Crisis (1956) in which he opposed Britain, and his attempts to solve the problem of the Congo (now Zaire) were attacked by the Soviet Union. In pursuit of the solution there he was killed when his plane crashed, aged fifty-six. He was unmarried.

His private journal of notes and poems, translated by W. H. Auden and published under the title *Markings* (1964), reveal an intensely religious soul but one outside the orbit of any organized religion. A strong sense of dedication is at the centre of his life. It stems from a feeling of relationship with God, a personal call to which he accepted gradually but decisively:

I don't know who – or what – put the question,
I don't know when it was put, I don't even remember
    answering.
But at some moment I did answer Yes to Someone or
    Something.
And from that hour I was certain that existence is meaningful
And that, therefore, my life, in self-surrender, has a goal.

The life of Dag Hammarskjöld, both his inner or spiritual life and the course of his career in the world, is enough to scotch the idea that the blessing of a vocation confers any special privileges. The path of demanding service is thorny and uphill, and it may require the acceptance of loneliness and personal self-sacrifice.

The Case of the Lakeland Poet

William Wordsworth was born at Cockermouth in Cumberland and educated at Hawkshead school and at St John's College, Cambridge. Going to France in 1791, he sympathized deeply with the revolutionaries, and fell in love with Marie-Anne Vallon, by whom he had an illegitimate daughter. Returning to England just before the Terror he published his first poems in 1793. Six years later he settled at Grasmere, and in 1802 married Mary Hutchinson. He finished the long autobiographical poem entitled *The Prelude* in 1805, when he was thirty-five years old, but it remained unpublished until 1850.

In a section about one summer's vacation from Cambridge, spent amid his beloved Cumbrian fells, he describes a whole night spent in 'dancing, gaiety and mirth' with others equally intent upon enjoying themselves. As dawn lightened the eastern sky he took the homeward path over the fells. It was a glorious sunrise, and he rejoiced in the effects of its light and the other sounds of the early morning. It was then that his calling, inseparable from this beauty all around him, became clear:

> *Ah! need I say, dear Friend! that to the brim*
> *My heart was full; I made no vows, but vows*
> *Were then made for me; bond unknown to me*
> *Was given, that I should be, else sinning greatly,*
> *A dedicated Spirit. On I walked*
> *In thankful blessedness, which yet survives.*

Perhaps no words in the English language better capture the essence of vocation than these. They are worth reflecting upon when you have a quiet moment.

The Few or the Many?

So far in this book the concept of vocation I have presented is a broad one, a net to catch everyone – including you! It is an open invitation. For I imagine vocation to be like the Caucus-race organized in *Alice in Wonderland*; at its end, as the Dodo announced after much thought: '*Everybody* has won, and *all* shall have prizes.'

But surely, that 'strange rendezvous', as Wordsworth called it, 'the memory of one particular hour' which stayed with him for ever, *is* limited to a few?

To be honest, I don't know the answer to that question. My intuition is that vocation is much more widely experienced, not least in retrospect, than is commonly believed.

While I served as Director of Studies at St George's House in Windsor Castle in 1968 I met the eminent scientist Professor Sir Alister Hardy, who told me about his plans to attempt an empirical study of religious experience. Subsequently he set up a trust to fund the Religious Experience Research Centre, as it became known, at Westminster College, Oxford.

Today that centre has a growing database – 1834 accounts to date – by individuals of their religious experience which are full-word searchable. Some 44 have in them the word *vocation*, though no accounts were assessed under *feel called* or *called*.

Perhaps it is uncommon for vocational people to have Wordsworth's sense of spiritual affirmation during or after they make their commitment. In any case, not everyone has quite that magnetic pull to a particular period of time and place – of the 'strange rendezvous' where the divine contract was recognized and accepted, just as not everyone can say when and where they fell in love with their life's partner. Much more common is the conviction that unpredictable 'providential accidents' have led the way, like the 'markings' – the cairns of stones that guide a mountain traveller – which gave Dag Hammarskjöld the title of his journal.

One Step Enough for Me

Sometimes those with religious faith do engage in listening prayer, seeking guidance in their vocation. For example, in 1832, when he was thirty-one years old and in considerable doubt about his course in life, John Henry Newman was travelling home by sea. On the sea passage home between Palermo and Marseilles, when his ship lay becalmed one night, he wrote down his heart's prayer in the form of a poem:

> Lead, kindly light, amid the encircling gloom,
> Lead thou me on;
> The night is dark, and I am far from home,
> Lead thou me on.
> Keep thou my feet; I do not ask to see
> The distant scene; one step enough for me.

To take your journey forwards one step at a time is, especially when visibility is poor, the vocational approach. 'The chain of destiny', said Winston Churchill, 'can only be forged one link at a time.'

It follows that in your quest for vocation – and as you steer to the next beacon – you will need, as a creative person, what John Keats called *negative capability*:

> At once it struck me what quality went to make a man of achievement, and which Shakespeare possessed so enormously – I mean negative capability, that is when a man is capable of being in uncertainties, mysteries, doubts, without any irritable reaching after fact and reason.

In other words, when you have fulfilled all the necessary conditions you may have to wait – to wait patiently and perhaps, if so inclined, prayerfully – for that mysterious sufficient condition to slide into place in the combination lock of vocation. By 'waiting' I don't mean doing nothing, far from it. It is when we are on the journey – actively seeking the way ahead – that the 'bond unknown' is suddenly given and then you walk on into the uncertain future with the unshakeable sense that you have found your calling in life.

CHECKLIST – Do You Have a Clear Sense of Direction?

Have you identified an aim in your life as far as your working career is concerned?

If so, does it match in sense – not word-for-word – the vocational aim set out in this chapter?

Have you a vision for your life?

'You can have one broad integrating purpose in life, which can be broken down into a number of aims – open-ended but directional'. Do you agree?

At the outset of your career, have you established the criteria by which you will judge your work?

If so, is the touchstone of vocation – how effectively you have used your abilities for good – at the top of the list?

Summary of Key Points

- In order to find and follow your vocation you will need to think clearly about your future life. Clear thinking doesn't come easy. You will probably find that you have to struggle to reach the necessary clarity.
- Purpose, Aims, Objectives and Steps (Fig. 3.1) may be a useful framework for you to consider. Vocation, in the more specific sense of finding and doing the work you love, is a principal *aim*, not the chief *purpose* of your life.
- To be clear about your vocational aim in life is the first necessary condition you can fulfil. The vocational aim that

helps to give direction to what Shakespeare calls 'life's uncertain voyage' is to put one's distinctive or unique talent to work. 'To do good', said Sophocles, 'is man's most glorious task.'

- A second necessary condition is that you commit yourself wholeheartedly to that concept of work, so that it becomes *your* aim in life, developing naturally in your personality.

- The test of this vocational aim is whether or not it is robust enough to last your lifetime. Each term in the equation – interests, skills, needs, circumstances – may change, like the timbers being replaced in an old ship, but the overall aim remains as constant as a star.

- Vocation is a journey. Once you have crossed the Rubicon and committed yourself, you may not have to go far down the road – some further than others – before you experience that sufficient condition which gives you the inner confirmation that you have found your vocation. Or it has found you!

> *Those who have gone through the door have completed half their journey.*
>
> Italian Proverb

4

Choosing Your Course –
Making a Start

From the gods comes the saying 'Know thyself'.

Juvenal, *Satires* (2nd century)

Granted that you now have a clear vocational aim, you still have choices to make. In terms of the parable it is *as if* the Master in the story has now called you to him for the general briefing and receipt of the allotted talents: you have been given the broad direction and left in no doubt as to what is expected. He then departs to a far country – no telephone, e-mail or faxes, remember. In other words, you are now *on your own*. It's up to you to decide how you are going to use your talents. As the proverb says, *God gives us nuts, but you have to crack them yourself*.

In effect, you have to answer the question, '*How* am I going to make the best use of my talents to the general good?' I am assuming, again, that no angel has told you what you must do with your life, that you have complete freedom of choice. To choose freely in this way, it is worth reminding ourselves, is an opportunity and privilege enjoyed by relatively few people before the present generation and by no means all that many people in the world even today. Where do you begin?

The obvious place to start is to open the box that the Master has given you and take stock of your talents.

The First Lesson in Life

Pablo Casals, the great cellist, believed in the uniqueness and gift in everyone:

'When will we teach our children in school what they are? We should say to each of them: Do you know what you are? You are a marvel. You are unique. In all the world there is no other child exactly like you. In the millions of years that have passed there has never been another child like you – look at your body. What a wonder it is, your legs, your arms, your cunning fingers, the way you move. You could become a Shakespeare, a Michelangelo, a Beethoven. You have the capacity for anything. Yes, you are a marvel. And when you grow up can you then harm another who is like you a marvel?'

What Are My Talents?

I find it useful to explore *talent* under three headings: *aptitudes*, *interests* and *temperament*. Together they constitute what you or I have to offer, as compared to other people.

Not that I am assuming you will have a perfect picture of these three factors. How people acquire knowledge of themselves would take a book in itself. It starts at a very early age, as a child begins to explore its environment. Being social beings by nature, we both give and receive observations and comments on others. Patterns begin to take shape in this informal or formal feedback (for example, in school reports), and some general ideas gradually coalesce. We discover what we are good at and not so good at, what we like most and what we like less. Our natural profile of aptitudes, interests and temperament slowly emerges, to be tested and modified over time.

Aptitudes

Just as a reminder, your *aptitudes* are your natural abilities, what you are fitted for by disposition. In particular, an *aptitude* signifies *your capacity to learn or acquire a particular skill*. For example, supposing your aptitudes for music, languages and maths are very low. That doesn't mean you cannot enjoy singing in the bath, or embarrassing your companion by speaking in French in Calais, or doing your own accounts. But these activities should not form a substantial part of your professional work.

Aptitude, you recall, can usefully be distinguished from *skill*, which suggests both some form of learned knowledge and the ability to use that knowledge effectively and readily in execution or performance. This learned power of doing something competently only develops – or is developed – over a period of time.

There are various ways of categorizing aptitudes – mechanical, linguistic, artistic, musical, and so on. No one scheme of classifying them is to be preferred to another. Anyway, not all aptitudes can be classified or put into pigeonholes in such a neat way.

Having an aptitude obviously implies the likelihood of success in it, for you are working with the grain of the wood, not against it. As I have said above, the natural level of motivation balances the aptitude. Your *interest* will be engaged. In *The Taming of the Shrew* Shakespeare says:

> No *profit grows where no pleasure ta'en;*
> *In brief, sir, study what you most affect.*

Interests

Interests are also natural endowments. Moreover, they are extremely important clues in your personal quest to find your vocation.

In *interest* has been defined as a state of feeling in which you wish to pay particular attention to something. You might have an interest in, for example, old coins or military history or the ballet. They may not be labelled 'interests' in your mind; they may even fall below the status of a conscious interest, but these feelings divert you to look outwards at something beyond yourself.

The idea that our interests are part of our talent is not a familiar one. 'Talent', you may recall, originates from the Greek *talanton*, a balance for weighing precious metals. A natural disposition or interest is like an inclination of the scales. Your mind – or as Shakespeare said, 'what you most affect' – tilts one way rather than another, as if responding to a magnetic attraction. Hence my idea that an interest can be categorized as a form of talent.

Exercise

Make a list of your *three* principal interests, those which naturally draw your attention and upon which you have spent time and money.

Put a star by any which has lasted more than five years. Put two stars if the interest manifested itself before you were eighteen years old.

It's sometimes easier to know what doesn't interest you rather than what does. So now list three occupations for which you have zero interest.

The interests which are the gold and silver of vocation tend to be ones which manifest themselves in childhood or early in life, long before you have considered what career you will pursue. As Graham Greene wrote in *The Power and the Glory*, 'There is always one moment in childhood when the door opens and lets the future in.' Be that as it may, perceptive parents may sometimes discern the seeds of the future in the present interests of their children.

Temperament

I am tempted to call this *personality*, but personality could be taken to include aptitudes and interests, and I want to differentiate this third area a little more clearly.

As you will see, unlike the previous checklists the one below doesn't have blatantly 'right' answers! Yet it's difficult to give you much guidance in interpreting the results. I would stress the importance of honesty with yourself. Most of us like to see ourselves in a good light, and that desire may blind us to the realities of our temperaments. So we sometimes launch into careers for which – it appears later – we are not temperamentally suited.

Temperament, then, is obviously an integral part of your make-up and it is the most difficult aspect of yourself to change. As a commonsense general principle it is best to work within the compass of your temperament – which is not to say that you shouldn't try to control its less helpful elements!

For when it comes to temperament it's important to remember that it's all about *tendencies*. To describe someone as temperamentally lazy only means that he or she has a *tendency* to be lazy. To be quick-tempered or aggressive doesn't mean to say that you always lose your temper or seem to attack people.

Therefore you should always be cautious about using your temperament as an excuse for not doing what you should do or doing what you shouldn't do. When her son told the author Dorothy Sayers that he was temporarily separated from his wife, blaming his explosive temperament, she replied with a long letter of rebuke:

> I know all about 'temperament'; it is the word we use for our own egotism, and, for our own bad temper and bad manners – and the mere fact that we use the word implies that we intend to take no serious trouble to control ourselves ... Let me hear that you have made it up with Jeanne, for whom I have every sympathy.

CHECKLIST – Some Temperamental Factors

What kind of vocational field best suits you? Consider such questions as the following:

Do you prefer working with others rather than on your own?

Would you rather lead a team than take instructions?

Would you describe yourself more as at the introvert than the extrovert end of the spectrum?

Or are you somewhere in the middle ground – an ambivert?

Are you inclined to indecision?

Would you say you tended to be naturally lazy?

Would you describe yourself as very cautious and risk-averse?

Can you work in a stressful environment?

Do you work best with the pressure of deadlines?

What are the five adjectives most commonly used by others who know you well to describe your temperament?

Do you prefer to work more out of doors or more indoors?

Are you happy to do repetitive work or routine adminis-tration?

How important is variety and challenge to you?

Is the prospect of promotion to higher responsibility essen-tial for you?

Are you naturally competitive?

In what ways does your present job, if you have one, not suit your temperament?

Having achieved a working knowledge of your aptitudes, interests and temperament – the solicited or unsolicited comments of others who know you can be immensely helpful here – the next step is to list your options.

Identifying the Feasible Options

Notice that word – 'options' rather than 'alternatives'. An alternative is literally one of two courses open. Decision-makers who lack skill tend to jump far too quickly to either-or-alternatives. They do not give enough time and mental energy to generating at least three or four possibilities. In the Parable of the Talents the 'unprofitable servant' was criticised by the Master because he had not considered all the alternatives. As Bismarck used to say to his generals, 'You can be sure that if the enemy has only two courses of action open to him, he will choose the third.' Alfred Sloan, the renowned President of General Motors, was even known to adjourn board meetings in which he was presented with two alternatives. 'Please go away and generate more options,' he would say to the startled directors.

Look at the Lobster Pot Model (Figure 4.1). As it suggests, you need to open your mind into wide focus to consider all possibilities, and that is where creative thinking comes in. But then your valuing faculty must come into play in order to identify the feasible options. '*Feasible*' means capable of being

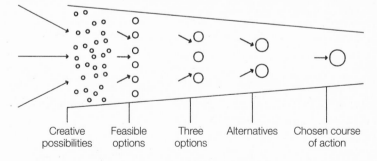

| Creative possibilities | Feasible options | Three options | Alternatives | Chosen course of action |

Figure 4.1 The Lobster Pot Model

done or carried out or realized. If an option is feasible it has some real likelihood of being workable. It can attain the end you have in mind.

In the vocational context the feasible options are the ones accessible to you *now* or in the near future in terms of age and paper qualification requirements. Equally important, these occupations hold out the promise that they will engage your natural interests and employ your natural aptitudes, so that you might well expect to be successful in that respect too. I am not thinking in the first instance of promotion, which is a separate issue. On the other hand, if you are temperamentally strongly ambitious, then promotional prospects are something to take into account.

Exercise

Assuming that you are in a situation for vocational choice, either now or imminently, write down the *feasible* options, taking all factors into consideration. The list can be as short or as long as you wish.

CAREER CHOICE	WHY IS IT FEASIBLE FOR YOU?

It is worth spending a bit of time – possibly on research in the library or asking around – to see if you have identified all the feasible options. Watch out for assumptions that may, on examination, prove to be false, such as 'I am too old to become a vet.' That may or may not be true. Check it out with all the veterinary science colleges – there may be one without an official or unofficial age qualification. Don't take No for an answer until it really is No.

Having now made a list of your *feasible* options, the next step is to eliminate the less attractive ones.

Narrowing Down the List

Karl Popper, the eminent philosopher, points out that in science it is virtually impossible to *verify* anything; what you can do, however, is to *falsify* proportions. In vocational choice situations the same is true. It is usually easier to establish that one course or career is *not* suitable or is unlikely to be successful in terms of your vocational aim than to discover what is the right one.

How can this process of elimination be carried out? What you need to do is to *gather more information*. Here are some possibilities for doing so:

- *Using your imagination.* Removing your 'rose-tinted spectacles', picture yourself in the characteristic working situations of the profession or trade you have in mind. Obviously the more you know about that occupation the more realistic this self-projection will be. Beware of wanting to *be* something – a politician for example – but not to *do* the work. Still interested?
- *Ask a practitioner or two.* Informally 'interviewing' a few people already engaged in that job is usually revealing. Do it in their place of work if possible. Remember, however, to *choose vocational people*, those who love the work. Compared to the others you will actually find them *more* truthful about the realities of the work. They will tell you where the shoe pinches. Are they the sort of people you can naturally accept as 'role models'? Do you feel really put off by what they say?
- *Have a trial.* Sometimes you can test a precarious-looking footbridge without committing yourself to cross it. If time and circumstances allow, try to get some experience of the work and see what it is like. As the old military proverb affirms, time spent on reconnaissance is seldom wasted.

You have now only two or three feasible options left on the list. As you have sieved out the less value-laden ones, for one good vocational reason or another, those you are left with may present you with a difficult choice. How do you decide?

Usually the trick is to go on accumulating and piling *information* about the two (or three) options into the scale-pans, and gradually you will find that one side moves down. The decision, if you like, is making itself. It is as if you flow in one direction and not in the other, and – noticing this direction – you say to yourself, 'I have decided.'

If you are really stuck, sleep on it – allow your depth mind to do its work. As we all know, we have subconscious and unconscious minds. But we are not so aware of the vital part that these dimensions – I call them the 'depth mind' – play in our thinking. You can actually analyse, synthesize, and value in your sleep or when you are consciously doing something quite different, like gardening or washing the dishes. Far from being chaotic, the depth mind plays a large part in scientific discovery and creative art. It is also the source of intuition, that all-important sixth sense. Roy Thompson, in his autobiography *After I was Sixty* (1975), explains how it works:

> When a new problem arose, I would think it over and, if the answer was not immediately apparent, I would let it go for a while, and it was as if it went the rounds of the brain cells looking for guidance that could be retrieved, for by the next morning, when I examined the problem again, more often than not the solution came up right away. That judgement seems to have come to me almost unconsciously considering the problem, my subconscious had been turning it over and relating it to my memory.

It is worth keeping the channel open to your depth mind throughout your life. You never know when, for example, it may whisper in your ear that you are in a rut, or that you are missing an opportunity to move forwards in a slightly different direction.

Freud's Decision-Making Strategy

In a psychoanalytic session the other day, I controlled the impulse to remark, 'When I was five and twenty, I heard a wise old man say . . .' A young man had come to consult me about two decisions that he had to make: should he follow a certain profession and ought he to marry a certain girl. Something in him or in his situation reminded me of myself at his age. He had just received his doctorate in psychology. I, too, had won my PhD at this age and I was a student of Freud.

One evening I ran into the great man on his daily walk along the Ringstrasse in Vienna, and walked home with him. Friendly as always, he asked me about my plans and I told him of my problems, which resembled those of my present patient. Of course, I hoped Freud would give me advice or resolve my doubts.

'I can only tell you of my personal experience,' he said. 'When making a decision of minor importance, I have always found it advantageous to consider all the pros and cons. In vital matters, however, such as the choice of a mate or a profession, the decision should come from the unconscious, from somewhere within ourselves. In the important decisions of our personal life, we should be governed, I think, by the deep inner needs of our nature.'

Without telling me what to do Freud had helped me make my own decision. Like marriage, the choice of a profession is a matter of destiny. We should welcome our destiny, readily accepting what comes with and out of it. On that evening thirty-five years ago when I decided to become a psychoanalyst, I married the profession for better or for worse.

Dr Theodor Reik, *Listening with the Third Ear*

The Trial-and-Error Strategy

Trial and error is a way of finding out the best way to reach a desired result or a correct solution by trying out one or more ways or means and by noting and eliminating errors or courses of failure. More loosely, it means the trying of this and that until something succeeds.

When applied to finding your vocation, this strategy has the drawback that it is very time-consuming. On the other hand, the experience gained in the 'false starts' can be put to use – a theme I shall explore in the next chapter.

You cannot avoid experience – actually testing it out by doing it – in your quest for vocation. There is no such thing as armchair vocation. The aim of this chapter is to ensure that you do not expend too much time in fields where you are a misfit. I speak from experience – it's easily done!

Using these techniques you should be able to make an intelligent choice of a 'front runner'. That doesn't mean to say it's right for you. At least you will be more or less in the right field. But remember that it is still a *hypothesis*. Your vocation may well be in that direction, but until you have tried it you will not know for sure.

If you adopt this experimental approach, even after you have made your decision and initially committed yourself, your depth mind will soon give you signs if you are on the wrong course.

Beware of giving up too easily – all vocations are daunting in their early stages. But if it isn't for you, stay calm and politely but firmly part company. Cut your losses. You haven't failed – you have just eliminated one possibility.

Before Edison achieved success in inventing the light bulb, a newspaper reporter asked him, 'Why do you persist in spending all this time and money when you have failed so many times?' 'Young man,' Edison replied, 'you don't understand how this world works! I have not failed. I have successfully discovered over 100 ways that do not work. That puts me over 100 ways closer to the way which does!'

On Changing Horses in Midstream

You may not have had the benefit – such as it is – of reading this book when you were on the threshold of life. So it's just possible that you may be engaged upon a career that you now suspect is not your true vocation.

Checklist – Are You in Your True Vocation?

Would you describe yourself as chronically discontented with your work?

If it was not for the money, would you take early retirement tomorrow if it was offered to you?

Has all the fun and enjoyment gone out of daily work?

Has anyone said to you in the last year 'I think you are in the wrong job,' or words to that effect?

If you could start your career all over again would you choose what you are doing today?

Do the factors you dislike about your job outweigh the ones you like?

Are the positive ones more to do with extrinsic rewards – salary, status and lifestyle – rather than intrinsic factors, such as interest, challenge and stimulating colleagues?

If you have answered Yes to most of these questions, you then need to assess other elements of your situation. How committed are you to the present set-up for financial reasons? How supportive would your spouse or partner be if you decided to make a change? Have you a feasible option, one which would better align you with your new vocational aim? What are the costs of transferring to it? Is the *value* of finding your true vocation worth the price you will have to pay?

For one reason or another, you may not be free – or feel free – to follow your star. Let us look at some of these possible barriers.

Other People

Other people – parents, relatives, teachers, friends, superiors – may have strong views about what you should do with your life. Listen to what they say, even if it is unsolicited advice, for they know you (in part, perhaps) and the world – or some of it. But the responsibility is yours alone for answering the vocational question: 'What shall I do with my life?'

If subtle pressure builds up and other forms of opposition develop, then stay calm and quietly determined to follow your own inner compass. You may get lost, but it will be *your* lostness. You don't want to live with the shadow of what-might-have-been.

Remember that vocational people are tenacious when facing difficulties. You are bound to face discouragement at some stage or other, although the worst is what comes from those dear to you. Yet it is vocation that sets your feet on the adventure of your life, and you cannot miss out on that. *'If you look behind you,'* says a proverb of the Australian Aborigines, *'you will never leave.'*

Lack of Freedom

What happens if, for some reason, you are not free to choose what you want to do? You may be committed to a domestic situation which requires your time and attention, or at least a good deal of it.

Or, probably because of financial and family commitments, you are saddled with your present job, whatever it is. Perhaps you work in a finance house, commuting daily into the city, but dream of working as a potter in Tuscany – for your real love is making pots. What if you cannot see a way out of your present circumstances? You may have come down the wrong road but – to mix metaphors – it is impossible to change horses in midstream. Are you condemned to frustration?

Not necessarily. Take a fresh look at your present situation and see what vocational possibilities, if any, it holds for you. You may not see them at once, but they may emerge after a time of reflection. Sometimes vocational people seem to transform their present situations in a creative and innovative way, even though these situations are not of their own choosing and are far from what the world might call favourable or promising.

The Role of Planning

'I've never planned a career. I have always tried to lead my life as a vocation and let things unfold,' says Terry Waite. When I first met Terry many years ago, he was a Church Army captain involved in adult education. He shot to prominence much later as a hostage held in Beirut by an extremist Arab group, seized while attempting to secure the release of other hostages. Not a career that anyone could have planned! It reminds me of the proverb: '*If you want to make God laugh, tell him your plans.*'

'Planning' may sometimes imply only a vague goal or an indefinite resolution that is not being presently acted upon. But to 'plan' may be, and often is, much more definite than to 'intend', implying the taking of active steps towards the realisation of an intention. Such planning involves a consideration of the ways and means of achieving a purpose, and the making of arrangements in advance.

The contrast in Terry Waite's mind between a *planned* career and an *unplanned* vocation is a common one, but it is now increasingly blurred. Careers are being slowly transformed into vocations. Each cannot be planned beyond a certain point and must be allowed to unfold.

'Career' – from the Latin *carraria*, a road for vehicles – does imply a structure. Progression usually means promotion, hence the core to a career is the *career ladder*. It answers the question,

'How do I get to the top?' There may be several routes to the summit but the goal is clear.

Not all make it to the top. Roman paved roads had deep ruts in them, carved out by countless chariot or carriage wheels. Some people, as they pursue their careers, find themselves in a rut – a route that doesn't seem to be leading anywhere. They do much the same each day but work begins to feel more and more like a monotonous routine. If so, it's time for a change. Sometimes getting out of a rut is the hardest mountain a person may ever have to climb in their quest for vocation.

There are some careers with clear hierarchies – for example, the civil service or the armed forces – where some career planning is still appropriate. But the impact of change – economic, social and technological – on most careers has been devastating. The likelihood of a person pursuing his or her whole career in one organization or institution is now low. Change throws up new demands and opportunities within traditional careers that cannot be foreseen and planned for. That is why I suggest that careers are increasingly beginning to look like vocations *and have to be lived as such*.

That doesn't mean to say that you shouldn't have a plan for finding your vocation or indeed a tentative one for pursuing it; indeed, it is essential to have both in order to make anything out of your life. But, with regard to the latter, as an Israeli general said, 'A plan is a very good basis for changing your mind.'

The best plans in such a fluid career situation as we now find are those which give us general *directions* rather than something that looks like a detailed map. What then matters is moving or making progress in those directions, even if we have to abandon the set roads and take to our feet across unexplored country.

'I try to edge my work in a direction that interests me and avoid stuff I'm sick of,' says the artist and illustrator David Gentleman. 'But I don't plan in any great strategic sense. You can't in this life.'

Chaos Theory

All human affairs are subject to an interdetermination principle. What happens five minutes from now is pretty well determined, but as that period is gradually lengthened a larger and larger number of purely accidental occurrences are included. Ultimately a point is reached beyond which events are more than half determined by accidents which have not yet happened. Present planning loses significance when that point is reached.

'On the Nature of Progress', a paper by
Professor H. P. Phillips of the
Massachusetts Institute of Technology (1945)

'Chaos Theory', as it is now called, suggests that all plans beyond a relatively short time frame will be like tracks that peter out in a jungle of unpredictable accidents, contingencies and opportunities.

Vocation, then, is an adventure. Your journey may be compared to walking down a long corridor through some open rooms.

This Corridor Model (Figure 4.2) illustrates how vision increases as your vocation progresses. The analogy is of someone who enters the room and can see all that room clearly.

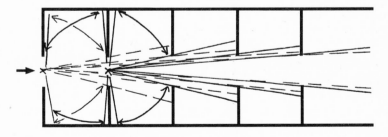

The Corridor Model

What lies beyond becomes progressively clearer as each threshold is approached (and, sometimes, what happened in the past becomes mercifully obscured!). In other words, our perspective in life – future, past and present – is constantly changing. As you move through the open rooms, other doors shut but other doors appear – doors of need or opportunity.

Checklist – Have You Made the Right Choice?

Have you a reasonably clear and objective idea of your aptitudes, interests and temperament?

Are you clear about the callings or professions for which you are *not* well fitted?

Have you spotted in yourself a key talent, one that is relatively uncommon?

Have you completed the exercise of identifying your feasible options and eliminating the others?

Do you have a friendly and positive attitude to your depth mind? Do you *expect* it to work?

Have you allowed in your work of charting your course for time to 'sleep on it', so as to give your depth mind an opportunity to contribute?

Have you experienced waking up next morning to find that your unconscious mind has resolved some problem or made some decision for you?

Do you now have a clear course of action before you, a vocational plan?

Summary of Key Points

- It is useful to have a decision-making framework in order to think clearly about the career choices you have to make.

This framework is important not only when you are facing your initial choice of vocation but also when you come to the major roundabouts on your journey with several feasible exits.

- The key factors in choosing your field of work are:

What are your interests?	An interest is a state of feeling in which you wish to pay particular attention to something. Long standing interests – those you naturally like – make it much easier to acquire knowledge and skills.
What are your aptitudes?	Aptitudes are your natural abilities, what you are fitted for by disposition. An aptitude is a capacity that may range from being a gift or talent to simply being above average.
What are the relevant factors in your temperament?	Temperament is an important factor. Some people, for example, are uncomfortable in decision-making situations of stress and danger, while others thrive on them.

- Having taken stock of your aptitudes, interests and temperament, brainstorm all the possible vocations. Then select five or six feasible options for further thought and research.
- The feasible options are the ones – given your talents and circumstances – that are capable of being done or carried out. What is possible is not always practicable. Because your time is limited you need to select what is likely to work out well in practice for you.
- It is always easier to eliminate – to know what you do *not* want to do. That's a useful way of narrowing down the choices.
- There are various ways of gathering information about these

options. After listing the pros and cons for each of them, weighted or illustrated by the facts or data you have accumulated, set a time limit and let your depth mind do the work for you. 'One should never impose one's views on a problem,' writes Albert Einstein. 'One should rather study it, and in time a solution will reveal itself.'

- Accept false starts as part of the trial-and-error process – learning the hard way! It is never unwise to turn back if you are on the wrong road. Don't regard such abandoned courses as failures – see them more as experiments. It all beds down, anyway, in the compost heap of experience. Even if inadvertently you turn your back on the way that leads to your vocation, all may not be lost. For, as a French proverb goes, '*A person often meets his destiny on the road he takes to avoid it*'.

- Planning should enable you to anticipate general developments and make some specific arrangements, such as going on a training course. Following a plan always entails taking some *definite steps*, as opposed to just drifting with the stream. Only dead fish do that. But remember the paramount need to balance persistence with flexibility.

Men sleep well in the Inn of Decision.
                                                          Arab proverb

5

The Creative Spirit

In dreams begin our possibilities.

William Shakespeare

What happens if Plan A to finding your vocation doesn't work? Plan A is roughly the rational decision-making approach – the Lobster Pot – that I outlined and discussed in the last chapter. It works pretty well when your vocation lies in an *existing* career, profession or trade. But what if you don't fit into any of the 'square holes' of existing occupations? Don't worry, you haven't missed the boat. You just have to make your own boat. That is Plan B.

The Parable of the Arab Dhow

In Dubai this afternoon, I walked along the busy quayside watching the dhow as it cruised in Dubai creek. It was like an old galleon shorn of its masts and powered by hidden engines. 'The builder of this dhow has no blueprint or plan on paper,' my host, a descendant of a family who once owned a fleet of pearl-fishing dhows, informed me. 'The plan was entirely in his head.'

I could not help wondering what sort of plan he had in mind. For a plan is a drawing or diagram done on a plane, hence its name. It may be a top or horizontal view of an object such as a house, or a large-scale map of a small area. By extension, making a plan always implies mental formulation and sometimes graphic representation. Plans are essentially methods of making or doing something or achieving an end.

William Wordsworth wrote a poem entitled 'Character of the Happy Warrior'. It begins:

> *Who is the Happy Warrior? Who is he*
> *That every man in arms should wish to be?*
> *It is the generous spirit, who, when brought*
> *Among the tasks of real life, hath wrought*
> *Upon the plan that pleased his boyish thought.*

If that 'plan' means having a complete blueprint in one's mind and bringing that concept into realization, then who indeed is the 'Happy Warrior'? But actually I doubt if the Arab shipwright's mental plan was quite like that. This afternoon I inspected some forty or fifty dhows. They were all broadly similar in shape but extraordinarily different in their actual designs and details. I suspect the Arab shipbuilder laid out the keep using what timber was available from India and then looked at it carefully, adapting his general 'dhow plan' to the realities of his materials and the pocket of his customer.

An Invitation to Creativity

'Man is preeminently a creative animal,' wrote Dostoevski, 'predestined to strive consciously for an object and to engage in building – that is, incessantly and eternally to make new roads, wherever they may lead.' If you cannot find your vocation, why not invent one for yourself? You have been given the timber: the natural shapes and sizes of your interests, aptitudes and personality. What can you make out of what you have been given? That is your vocational challenge. It calls for a special form of creativity.

For it is the creative spirit in you that can transform these raw materials at hand into a vocation that does 'add value' to society, however small a canvas you may have to work upon. You may need some outside help. Whether you call it luck or providence I'll leave to you. But it's amazing how much you can do with a little creative thinking.

How good are you as a creative thinker? Have you an open mind? Are you flexible and resourceful? You may like to test yourself by tackling the following exercises.

Problem 1 *The Nine Dots*

Take a piece of paper larger than this page and put on it a pattern of nine dots, like this:

● ● ●

● ● ●

● ● ●

Now connect up the dots by four straight consecutive lines (that is, without taking your pen or pencil off the paper). You should be able to complete this task within two minutes.

Problem 2 *The Six Matchsticks*

Place six matchsticks – preferably of the wooden variety – on a flat surface. Now arrange the matchsticks in a pattern of four equilateral (i.e. equal-sided) triangles. You may not break the matchsticks – that is the only rule. Again, you should be able to do it within two minutes. There are at least two solutions.

The well-known technique of 'brainstorming' challenges one kind of unconscious assumption, namely that hammers are for knocking in nails or that scissors are for cutting. But there are other forms of unconscious assumption that may inhibit your thinking.

Take the Nine Dots and Six Matchsticks problems you have just tackled. The reason why many people cannot do the first one is that they put an unconscious or invisible framework around the dots, and try to solve the problem within it. That is impossible. But if you break out of that self-imposed limitation, the solution to the problem is easily reached.

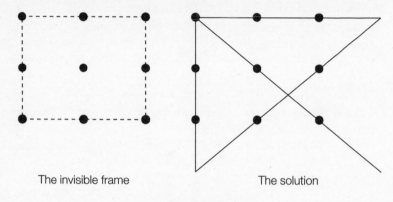

The invisible frame   The solution

The 'Nine Dots' solution

There is a similar assumption made in the second problem. People assume that they must arrange the six matches in a pattern of four equilateral triangles in only one plane. If they take one small step and give themselves permission to place matches on top of one another, they can reach the first solution. But if they break out of the two-dimensional constraint into three dimensions, they achieve the most elegant solution.

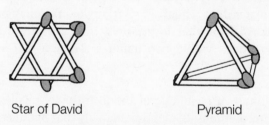

Star of David   Pyramid

The 'Six Matchsticks' solution

Please don't mistake me: you cannot think without making assumptions. But they should be conscious ones from which you can retreat when they become indefensible. The assumptions that trip you up are the unconscious ones, the constraints or limitations that you are not aware of. That is one reason why effective thinking needs social interaction. We need our brothers and sisters to remove these filters from our eyes.

Thinking Outside the Box

The Nine Dots Problem first appeared in one of my books, *Training for Decisions*, as long ago as 1969, and since then it has generated a new maxim in the English language – *think outside the box*. The 'box' in question is the unconscious framework imposed on the dots.

To be in the wrong box is to be in the wrong place. A box is a rigid structure. We do get boxed in – or box ourselves into – situations. Often the solution to our problem – in this case, finding true vocation – lies outside the existing career or occupational structures. If you are a young person, for example, your vocation may lie in an *occupation that does not at present exist*. It is still over the horizon.

Therefore, the fact that you haven't found your vocation yet is not proof that you will never find it. It may be advancing to meet you out of the mists of the future. What we call a *sense of destiny* is that feeling of being called or set aside for a task yet to be revealed. There is an unmistakable joy – a leaping of the heart within you – when that hour strikes. Like a nearly completed jigsaw puzzle, the separate parts and those apparently irrelevant early experiences of your life come together, and you see the face of your calling.

On the night of 10 May 1940, King George VI invited Winston Churchill to form a government and lead Britain against the forces of Nazism that threatened to dominate Europe and extinguish the light of democracy and civilization as we know it. The war situation was sombre, getting worse by the day. Yet Churchill was exalted. 'I felt as if I was walking with destiny,' he later recounted, 'and that all my past life had been but a preparation for this hour and for this trial.'

Few of us, it is true, are destined to play such unscripted parts on the stage of national and international history. But you can look laterally – outside the box – to see if you might make connections that no one has made before.

We cannot create out of nothing. One important way of *thinking outside the box* in the context of vocation is to look at what is left out of your present less-than-satisfactory job. You may find that you have interests or talents put away in the bottom drawer – or regarded as hobbies – which may be creatively woven into the pattern of your vocation.

Or, putting it another way, you may have more choices than you think you have for ways of fulfilling your vocational aim. Remember that vocation is not synonymous with paid employment. In the following cases I shall explore some of the different ways in which vocational people achieve the optimum in using all their talents within the limitations imposed upon them.

The Case of the Missionary Doctor

As an undergraduate at Cambridge I waited one day in 1958 outside the Senate House to see Albert Schweitzer emerge after receiving an honorary doctorate. Earlier that afternoon I had heard him play Bach chorales on the organ of King's College Chapel. It was a great day, for he was one of my boyhood heroes.

Born in 1875 in Alsace, Schweitzer achieved eminence as a theological scholar and organist. But he gave it up to train as a doctor and work in West Africa. In 1952 he was awarded the Nobel Peace Prize.

In vocational terms, Schweitzer had strong interests and talents: as a Christian pastor, as a scholar and as an organist. He also felt a call to active hands-on service to those in need – action as contrasted to talk. As a young man he reached a creative solution: he would pursue his vocation as scholar and artist until he was thirty, and his vocation to direct personal service from there on. This he did. In *My Life and Thought* (1933), he described his thought processes.

Even as a schoolboy and at university Schweitzer was acutely aware of the suffering encountered by others around him, in contrast to his own happy life. Thankfulness was the mainspring of his sense of vocation:

> Then one brilliant summer morning at Günsbach, during the Whitsuntide holidays – it was in 1896 – there came to me, as I awoke, the thought that I must not accept this happiness as a matter of course, but must give something in return for it. Proceeding to think the matter out at once with calm deliberation, while the birds were singing outside, I settled with myself before I got up, that I would consider myself justified in living till I was thirty for science and art, in order to devote myself from that time forward to the direct service of humanity. Many a time already I had tried to settle what meaning lay hidden for me in the saying of Jesus, 'Whosoever would save his life shall lose it, and whosoever shall lose his life for my sake and the Gospel's shall save it.' Now the answer was found. In addition to the outward, I now had inward happiness.
>
> What would be the character of the activities thus planned for the future was not yet clear to me. I left it to circumstances to guide me. One thing only was certain, that it must be directly human service, however inconspicuous the sphere of it.'

A long quest for a suitable form of service in Europe followed. It was not until six years after that morning at Günsbach, however, that an article in the magazine of the Paris Missionary Society entitled 'The Needs of the Congo Mission' caught his eye. It appealed for doctors and nurses.

> The writer expressed his hope that his appeal would bring some of those 'on whom the master's eyes already rested' to a decision to offer themselves for this urgent work. The conclusion ran: 'Men and women who can reply simply to the Master's call, "Lord, I am coming," those are the people whom the Church needs.' The article finished, I quietly began my work. My search was over.

There are three points worth considering from the story of Albert Schweitzer:

- Christian though he was, no divine voice spoke to Schweitzer, no angel told him what to do. Given his knowledge of his interests and aptitudes, his commitment to the Kingdom of God and his Buddha-like awareness of human pain and suffering, he had to work it out for himself.
- Schweitzer did have a vision for his life: or, if you prefer, he had a long-term view of it. Thus he was able to plan to use one set of talents up to the age of thirty, then switch to using another set thereafter. Rather than advance on a broad front, his vocational strategy was a sequential one – like two stages of a rocket.
- It is often through need – the perception of need – that the distinctive call comes. But you have to be ready for it. As Louis Pasteur said, 'Fortune favours the prepared mind.'

The Case of the Famous General

Eggs in a nest may look equal in size, shape and colour, but when the eaglets hatch one will tend to prove stronger than another. Normally you should choose the stronger talent as the core of your vocation, providing it doesn't totally exclude or eclipse the other talent. For your task is to develop and use *all* your talents, not to slaughter one of them on the altar of success.

Harold Alexander, first Earl Alexander of Tunis, was one of the few famous British generals of the Second World War. Commissioned into the Irish Guards he had served with distinction in the First World War. He was a natural soldier and a natural military leader, with all the qualities and attributes that soldiers admired and followed in their officers. He was known universally as 'Alex'.

In the First World War Alexander found his vocation as a soldier. After the war he sought out more opportunities to command in the Baltic States. The Second World War found him at the height of his powers. He held commands in France, England, Burma, North Africa and Italy, finishing the war as Supreme Allied Commander in the Mediterranean.

I met Field Marshal Lord Alexander once, in the last year of his life, in St George's House, a conference centre in Windsor Castle. He struck me, as he did others, as a reserved, rather withdrawn man. Nigel Nicholson's biography of him, *Alex* (1973), confirms that he was indeed self-effacing, and more than that – a man of humility.

Nicholson's biography also revealed that from boyhood Alexander had a talent as an artist, and contemplated becoming a professional artist – he even dreamed of becoming President of the Royal Academy. During the Second World War he found time to indulge his profound interest in painting. A professional artist who happened to be on Alexander's staff, Edward Seago, often accompanied him on these oil painting expeditions and became a close friend. In the biography mentioned above Seago writes of him:

If Alex had chosen to devote his whole time to painting he would have become a very good painter. I think he had all the instincts of a painter inside him. The amateur painter is very often pleased with something he's done. The professional is always disappointed. Churchill, to my mind, was the amateur of amateurs . . .

He had the attitude of a painter. What he lacked was time. You need years of practice before you can control your brush. You can't give it up for six months. You've got to go on and on. But his attitude was that of a professional. And he found painting the perfect relaxation, because when you are painting, you can't think of anything else but the picture, unlike gardening or driving, when you think about other things. If I said to some other amateurs, 'This is out of tone,' they wouldn't know what I was talking about, and so I wouldn't say it. It would spoil their fun. But Alex would.

Nigel Nicholson recalled a visit that Alexander paid to his Brigade headquarters in sight of the Alps in the Santerno valley towards the end of the Italian campaign. Alexander confided to the junior officers his vision of how the campaign might develop beyond the Alps, and then added: 'But what a pity it is to maul their beautiful country. I'll be glad when it's all over. I suppose they'll want me to govern some Dominion or other. But all I shall want to do is to paint and fish.'

Alexander painted all his life. After the war, as Governor General in Canada (he was right!) and then in retirement at home, he was at his most productive as an artist, and three times exhibited at the Royal Academy.

Was Alexander right to put soldiering first? Yes, because his natural talent for military leadership (and generalship) was strong. At his level, it is a much rarer talent than the ability to paint to a professional standard in oils. Both are gifts that Alex possessed, but one had a touch of being a gift about it, the sort that needs no self-advertisement. Alexander's painting served as recreation when his destiny appointed him to a leading role in the drama of the Second World War. Later, it moved more centre stage in the working out of his avocation.

The Case of the New England Poet

That word *avocation* I have just used stems from Protestant divines in the seventeenth century. Originally an avocation (from the Latin *avocare*, to call away) was something that diverted, distracted or took you away from your true vocation, but in the course of time it became just a synonym for vocation. Gradually it slipped out of common usage. But it is a word that deserves reinstating, for it is not a synonym. An avocation is a subordinate occupation pursued *in addition* to one's vocation, especially for enjoyment. In this latter sense it resembles a hobby or pastime, but with the suggestion of a much more dedicated pursuit. In other words, it has many elements of vocation in its own right.

Robert Frost was both a poet and a New England farmer.

He looked like a farmer. One day, when he was chopping logs, two men looking for work found him in the yard and offered to do it for money. Frost resisted the offer – he needed to do the work himself. In the poem which the incident inspired, he declares:

> *But yield who will to their separation,*
> *My object in living is to unite my avocation and vocation*
> *As my two eyes make one in sight.*
> *Only where love and need are one*
> *And work is play for mortal stakes*
> *Is the work ever really done*
> *For heaven and future's sake.*

Here Frost is using the words vocation and avocation in their correct senses. In his case there is a much closer and more creative relationship between two talents than in the case of Alexander. For as a poet who drew inspiration from nature, writing poetry and working with his hands out of doors in the changing seasons of New England are two sides of the same coin.

The Case of the Physician-Mountaineer

As his obituary in *The Times* (16 June 1999) reveals, Charles Warren coupled a lifelong love of mountains, literature and art with an eminent career in medicine. As a young and newly qualified houseman he gained leave from St Bartholomew's Hospital to join the three British attempts on Everest in the 1930s. He eventually became a specialist in paediatrics, renowned in his later career for performing exchange blood transfusions on infants with neonatal jaundice.

But beyond his medical career there remained his enduring delight in mountains and in the art and literature that they have inspired. He had a long association with the Wordsworth Trust at Dove Cottage, Grasmere, where he pursued his interest in the Romantic writers and poets – especially Wordsworth, Byron, Shelley and Mary Shelley – who visited the Alps and helped to form a fuller appreciation of them.

Warren was a man of relatively modest means, but his acquisitions as a collector demonstrated a shrewd eye for quality. He presented more than 200 items – including both texts and pictures relating to the Romantic movement – to the Wordsworth Trust.

'A kindly, good-humoured man,' *The Times* concludes, 'he wound the three strands of his interests – mountains, medicine and art – into a life of achievement.'

To combine three separate strands of interest and talent without losing focus and falling between all three stools is a challenge. The secret, as exemplified by Charles Warren, is to establish a firm base in one field, both professionally and financially. Then allow the other branches of your vocation, sustained from that trunk, to grow outwards and bear fruit.

The Case of the Egyptologist

Another obituary in *The Times* (23 July 1999) reveals an even more astonishing feat of creatively combining vocation and avocation. Jack Plumley managed to integrate a love of the parish ministry of the Church of England – he was ordained in 1933 – with leadership in the study of the language and archaeology of ancient Christian Egypt.

He owed his first interest in Egypt to a coppersmith grandfather who read him stories from Josephus, and to a Sunday School superintendent at Muswell Hill who had served in Egypt during the First World War.

He used his leisure hours to pursue Egyptian studies at University College, attending the lectures of Margaret Mead and Stephen Glanville. When the Blitz came he served his people through the worst of the bombing, visiting with a beaming and morale-raising smile the Underground stations used as vast dormitories.

During the air raids and among the stretchers over which people slept, he met a lonely Czech, then attached to the Czech Ministry of Foreign Affairs in Exile, Jaroslav Cerny. Plumley cared for this refugee from Hitler; and in return received from Cerny (who later became the Professor of Egyptology at London and then Oxford) the most expert private guidance in the subject which he still regarded as his hobby.

After the war, when he was vicar of St Paul's, Tottenham, he published a grammar of Coptic, the language of early Christian Egypt. This was at once indispensable, for example to students of the earliest monks and nuns, many whom wrote Coptic. His teacher Stephen Glanville became Professor of Egyptology at Cambridge and Provost of King's and persuaded the college to appoint Plumley rector at Milton outside Cambridge, with the idea that he could be useful to Glanville academically. Soon, in addition to his parish, where he served from 1947 to 1957, he was helping students with Coptic studies and was then made the secretary of the Oriental Languages faculty in the University.

When Glanville died prematurely, Plumley was elected to the chair. Although it was a wrench to give up the parish, he continued to help numerous churches and his college chapel. When he eventually retired as Professor of Egyptology, he continued his visits to Egypt and his care for the modern Coptics. But he also had time to become again a parish priest, of the little village of Longstowe, where they loved to have him as their pastor.

It is interesting to reflect on whether Plumley's life would have taken the course it did without that apparently chance meeting with Jaroslav Cerny in an air raid shelter during the London Blitz. Can you think of such 'providential accidents' in your own life story?

Had Plumley followed a purely secular interest – say Roman fortifications – the dissonance between vocation (which implies single-minded dedication) and avocation would have been too great – not a creative tension, but a conflict of interests. He would have had to choose between Church and World, not unlike those Egyptian hermits who engaged him so much. But the fact that his interest lay in *Christian* early Egyptian archaeology allowed him to preserve his integrity. The avocation, which he had expected to remain as such, unexpectedly was offered to him as his vocation, and what he had thought of as being his vocation now took second place.

The Case of the Plumber Who Collects Fossils

One man's obsession with fossil collecting has opened a window on the lost world of Britain's Jurassic past. Steve Etches, a plumber who left school without a qualification to his name, has single-handedly repopulated Britain's ancient seas with giant carnivorous reptiles, strange fish and swarms of swimming molluscs.

Until recently geologists had little idea of the variety of creatures in the seas around and over Britain in the Jurassic era 150 million years ago. Mr Etches has changed that by studying the Kimmeridge Clay, long neglected because it was believed to contain few fossils of interest. Deposited across northern Europe in the Jurassic era, it was considered of importance mainly because of its oil. Mr Etches, 49, just took an interest in fossils in his later twenties and decided to concentrate on the Kimmeridge Clay rather than the easy pickings at well-known sites such as Lyme Regis. Named after the Dorset village where he now lives, the clay is exposed in the cliffs and beaches of the area.

The tropical Jurassic sea was deep and perfectly calm at the bottom, and a steady rain of sediment quickly buried the dead creatures that sank there. Some fossils are remarkably well preserved, even the soft parts normally lost, such as the ink sacs of squid and a ray's wings. By developing his own techniques and using compressed air tools, Mr Etches was able to recover them from their shale shell.

The fossils include the two-metre jawbone of a pliosaur, the largest carnivorous reptile known to have lived, entire lobsters, sharks, turtles and shoals of beautifully preserved fish and fossil ammonities. The bones reveal a world in which the largest got larger and everything else got eaten. Almost every bone shows signs of having been someone's dinner.

Mr Etches, who moved to Kimmeridge to be closer the deposits, said: 'I was going around to museums telling them that what they thought were scratches were tooth marks. Until I came along, this record of predation went almost unnoticed. Now everyone can see it.'

Although he is consulted by palaeontologists from around the world, for five days a week he installs central heating systems. One day he hopes to open his collection to the public and work on his scientific papers, but he has to earn a living.

He says that his wife, Sue, and three children have no interests in fossils and think he is mad. Too often they have had to help him carry some promising-looking boulder back to his workshop.

Mr Etches has two regrets: 'That I didn't begin collecting fossils earlier and that I can't afford to devote all my time to them. That is what I really have a gift for.'

Simon de Bruxelles, *The Times* 20 August 1999

Steve Etches has found his vocation. Being a plumber is probably not so much an avocation, more a means of supporting himself and his family.

The Case of the Deaf Schoolmaster

The value of having or developing an avocation comes to the fore if ill-health prevents you from pursuing your primary vocation. By his mid-thirties Colin Dexter had risen to become Classics department head of a school in Corby, Northamptonshire, as he told Catherine O'Brian in an interview printed in *The Times* (14 July 2000).

He suspects he would still be there had he not suffered what
he calls the 'great good fortune' of going deaf. The hearing
loss was gradual, but by the time his job became untenable,
he had a wife and two children to support. So he embarked
on a second career, as a GCE examiner for the Oxford
University Board. 'I don't think that I would ever have been
tempted to write had I not moved here,' he muses. 'It was
never the idea of murders and police work that inspired me,
it was living in such a lovely city.'

Colin Dexter's brainchild Inspector Morse led to one of the
most successful detective series in TV history (750 million
viewers in 50 countries) and it has brought him fame and
riches. But Dexter would genuinely prefer that history
remembered him as a schoolmaster rather than an author. In
other words, his vocation – long-abandoned through deafness
– still comes first in esteem over his avocation, enjoyable and
profitable though that may have been.

> 'Being respected in the classroom has brought me more
> delight than anything else in my life, much more so than
> writing,' he says. 'People have sent me very moving letters
> about the Morse novels. They have described being desper-
> ately ill in hospital, thinking they weren't going to pull
> through, until their husbands brought them one of my
> books. All that is lovely, but, in a way, it is on a lower level
> than a career in education. As a teacher, if you are good,
> you stretch and broaden minds. You work them hard and
> take them that bit higher. And that is very gratifying.'

So, Take a More Creative Look at Yourself and Your Situation

Dorothy Sayers once observed, 'The artist does not see life as
a problem to be solved, but as a medium for creation.'

Eskimo artists, when they carve ivory, do not begin by decid-
ing what to carve. They say, 'I wonder what is inside.' As they

carve, they gradually find it. It is as if it was there, waiting for discovery and release.

Creative imagination is seeing the possibilities of the materials you have to offer: as circumstances change, so new problems arise. Look on these changes – often unplanned and unwanted – as opportunities, not problems. They are challenges to the creative spirit within you

> *Midway upon the journey of our life*
> *I found myself within a forest dark,*
> *For the straightforward path had been lost.*

You may know the feeling! These famous opening lines of Dante's *Il Paradiso* came to my mind when a fellow guest at a dinner to welcome in the new millennium told me his tale.

Richard had just been made redundant after working for twenty years as a geo-physicist for British Petroleum. With a group of colleagues he has been trying to get work as a consultant to the oil industry, but competition is stiff and business is hard to come by. His other major interest is archaeology, and he is presently working for two days a week as a volunteer for the local archaeological society.

Why not, I asked, combine the two? There are firms, Richard confirmed, specializing in archaeological geo-physics, but he had not considered that option seriously. He promised to explore it further. To me, having almost finished this book when we talked, it looks an obvious overlapping of two fields where his niche could well lie.

The great thing about vocation, if I may remind you, is not to sit down and wait to be called. Wait actively, on the principle that *God helps those who help themselves*.

The title of this book may be misleading in this respect. It suggests that your vocation lies there waiting for you to find it, like buried treasure somewhere under a ploughed field.

Now that notion – whether true or false – is operationally useful. In science, for example, the belief that there is such a thing as truth, and that it can be discovered by intelligent and

patient effort, has been extraordinarily productive. If scientists
had waited for philosophers to establish these propositions
before embarking on their unended saga of scientific discovery,
they would have remained tied up in harbour for ever. The
belief that something is *there*, if only I could discover it, is
actually operationally useful. It is as if there is a magnet pulling
you in that direction.

That is one face of the vocation. The other side of the coin
is that you may be invited to create your own vocation, or at
least to lend a hand in its creation. It cannot *find* it, you *make*
it. You are given the raw materials – the sum of what you are
and, sometimes but not always, a ready-made profession, trade
or occupation. But it is the creative spirit in you that transforms
that occupation into a vocation.

The Parable of the Fishing Net

When I was twenty I trained to be a deep-sea fisherman, learning among other things to make nets so that I would also know
how to repair them. Nets are not rigid things like ladders. They
are flexible, and you can catch fish in them. I never found a
way making a career ladder – or even the organisational box
I was searching for at the time – but I came to see later that
making a fishing net is a symbol of what happens in a vocation.
You weave together the unfolding threads – those three inter-
twined strands of interest, aptitude and temperament – to make
*something that will serve the most useful purpose you can
conceive*, given those raw materials.

The threads you are sent are not all silver or golden. You
may have to weave in misfortune or ill-health, or aspects of
your temperament which are otherwise than you would wish.
But it is essentially a creative process, which is what makes it
fun, a kind of adventure. You miss stitches, lose the thread,
spend time unravelling tangled situations, pierce your fingers
with the needle, abandon the work, go back to it and – turning
the tapestry to the light you see a pattern emerging. It bears
some resemblance to that lost pattern of what God had in

mind, though you seem to have been making it up as you go along!

For a web begun, God sends thread.
Italian proverb

There are actually a limited number of fishing-net designs, but look at any one and it is different. There are, I am told, only seven basic patterns of snowflake, but each flake is unique.

Even if you *are* following an established profession or career – most of us do – you can still weave the net in your own unique way, so that it both fulfils its functions and expresses *you*. Unlike paintings, books or pots, you do not add a signature to a fishing net: this fishing net *is* you.

Follow Your Inner Compass

Vocation is best compared to an adventurous journey into the unknown, one that calls for resourcefulness and creativity as well as the qualities of initiative, moral courage and perseverance. As a wayfarer, you will come upon obstacles in your path, risks to be assessed and even dangers.

Sometimes over-caution can obscure the path which, in our heart of hearts, we know to be the right one for us. As Shakespeare wrote:

> *Our doubts are traitors*
> *And make us lose the good we oft might will*
> *By fearing to attempt.*

The remedy then is to summon up some moral courage, and put your doubts to the test. 'If only' . . . 'What might have been' . . . 'If I had my time again': these are sad phrases. At least you will have tried! Take some advice from Rat in Kenneth Graham's *The Wind in the Willows*: 'Take the Adventure, heed the call, now ere the irrevocable moment passes! 'Tis but the

The Spirit of Adventure

'But if adventure has a final and all-embracing motive, it is surely this: we go out because it is in our nature to go out, to climb the mountains and sail the seas, to fly to the planets and plunge into the depths of the oceans. By doing these things, we make touch with something outside or behind, which strangely seems to approve our doing them. We extend our horizon, we expand our being, we revel in a mastery of ourselves which gives an impression, mainly illusory, that we are masters of our world. In a word, we are men, and when man ceases to do these things, he is no longer man.'

Wilfred Noyce, *Mountains and Men* (1947)

banging on the door behind you, a blithesome step forward, and you are out of the old life and into the new!'

'Did you ever get lost, having no compass?' a lady once asked the famous Kentuckian frontiersman Daniel Boone, who spent many weeks and even months wandering in the vast, trackless and unmapped wilderness.

'No,' he replied, 'I can't say as ever I was lost, but *I was once bewildered for three days.*'

If you have found your vocation you will never be totally unable to find the way, still less lost in the sense of being ruined or destroyed. But you may well sometimes find yourself perplexed or confused, perhaps by the very variety of choices before you but more often because you are temporarily 'bewildered'.

Bewilderment is a state of mind, a disturbing confusion in a situation which prevents clear thinking. It can be dispelled only by remaining calm and collected, so that your mind can think clearly.

The first thing to do is to take your bearings on fixed points, so that you can establish where you are. The fixed points in vocation are its planet-values. As with the brightest stars in the night sky, the darkness only makes them shine more brightly. Look up at them and remind yourself of your unchanging vocational purpose in life: to use all your talents and abilities in the love of service of something higher or more valuable than yourself.

Those twin values of *service* and *creativity* then come into view. Which of the paths before me will lead to *greater* opportunity to use my abilities in a creative way?

As a general principle in vocation, the rarer has precedence over the more common. If one of the paths before you is open to comparatively many people in your field, and is not short of 'takers', whilst the other is only takeable by a few – and you seem to be qualified – that is most probably the path for you.

The children's author Arthur Ransome advised others to 'follow your inner compass'. As you may recall, that compass-like sense of direction is a function of your depth mind, the largely unconscious part of your mind that is capable of analysing, synthesizing and valuing work. Intuition – the awareness that a situation exists when there is apparently no evidence for it – is another such function. What is happening here is that your mind is picking up signals through your five senses which are passed directly to the unconscious mind. After a period of incubation, some conclusion – a thought, clue or brainwave – enters the conscious mind as if 'out of the blue'. *This* way, not that, is the one for me.

If you consult your inner compass – not just once but on different days and in different moods – it will point in a certain direction. That may not be in the direction where those around you are heading; it may not even be towards any known career.

So you need some courage to step into the unknown, trusting in your compass. You may be completely wrong – the biggest error of your life. Or if you do make the right decision, you may never be absolutely certain that it was the right one. But more likely, you will have made the right decision. In the course of time, the elusive butterfly of vocation that seemed to be forever disappearing, will eventually come back to rest upon your shoulder. After stumbling through the wood in the dark, the dawn reveals that you are indeed on the right path.

Looking back with hindsight, you may be aware that at some point – you may never be quite sure when – you *did* make that momentous choice. The unpromising path, the one that you had to travel alone, proved against all the odds to be the right one for you. Robert Frost writes of such an experience in his poem 'The Road Not Taken':

> *I shall be telling this with a sigh*
> *Somewhere ages and ages hence;*
> *Two roads diverged in a wood, and I,*
> *I took the one less travelled by –*
> *And that has made all the difference.*

The Parable of the Poet

I have borrowed the title of this chapter from that given by C. Day Lewis, the former Poet Laureate, to an address he gave in Great St Mary's Church, Cambridge in 1971. In it he suggests that there is an analogy between the dependence of the poet on inspiration and that of *all* vocational people. Vocational people can fulfil all the necessary conditions to find their vocation, but there has to be something *given*. That gift or grace comes, as it were, from outside oneself: no amount of thought or common sense would have suggested it. You can wait, prepare and – if so inclined – pray for it, but you cannot command it. Here is the *sufficient condition*, the matchstick that is not in your hand. The analogy in the poet's life is the role that inspiration plays.

C. Day Lewis quoted the saying, 'Art is a house that tries to be haunted.' The work of the artist is to create the necessary conditions for this inspiration to happen: 'Every art is both an art and a craft. In painting, in music, in poetry, the practitioner is committed to a lifelong struggle with his medium: but he knows that all this devotion, all this perseverance cannot guarantee success – they can only make it possible – make it possible

for the mysterious X to enter into a work and inhabit there.'
The artist, continued Lewis, is a singularly fortunate person.

He is fortunate in his vocation – in being a person wide
open to creative spirit. He is fortunate because, on however
infinitesimal a scale, he is doing the work of creation; brood-
ing over a chaos of formless energy – memories, thoughts,
feelings, images – and making a pattern of it, reducing it to
order. He recognises himself as a man under authority – like
Robert Browning's poet:

> *Through a whole campaign of the world's life and*
> *   death*
> *Doing the King's work all the dim day long.*

The instinct to make something grow – a table, a baby, a
garden trellis or a scientific hypothesis – we know to be
universal, however humble or exalted the thing made, however ephemeral or long lived, it has come into being through
the operation of the creative spirit. It is possible, and right,
to take pride in what is a work of many hands – a controlled
experiment, a ship, an aircraft. From such working units,
the artist differs because his work is solitary: because it is
solitary, it can tempt him to satanic egotism; because his
ideal is perfection, he is often in danger of falling into
despair. If he avoids these dangers, it is because the spirit
which commands him to create also demands that he shall
communicate. The man who calls his wife into the workshop
and says, 'Look what I've made,' is following the same
impulse as the poet who hands a friend a finished poem and
asks, 'Have I made something of it?'

Lewis suggested that three qualities are required in a creative
or vocational person: patience, joy and disinterestedness. He
concluded with a poem 'Final Instructions' which used the
image of the preparations for an ancient ritual sacrifice as a
metaphor for the work of creating the necessary conditions to
attract inspiration. What must be offered is your best, but even

your best will by no means always be found acceptable. Don't be discouraged, however, for some passing lizard or cat may taste your sacrifice 'and bless the god'.

But the crucial point is this:
You are called only to *make* the sacrifice:
Whether or no he enters into it
Is the god's affair; and whatever the handbooks say,
You can neither command his presence nor explain it –
All you can do is to make it possible.

If the sacrifice catches fire of its own accord
On the altar, well and good. But do not
Flatter yourself that discipline and devotion
Have wrought the miracle: they have only allowed it.

So luck is all I can wish you, or need wish you.
And every time you prepare to lay yourself
On the altar and offer again what you have to offer,
Remember, my son,
Those words – patience, joy, disinterestedness.

Summary of Key Points

- 'Plans get you into things,' said the American humourist Will Rogers, 'but you got to work your way out.' Working your way out – working out your vocation for yourself – is not always an easy matter. It calls for imagination, patience and perseverance.
- As the four case studies show, vocations are made creatively, like fishing nets, from all the interests and aptitudes we have to offer. Usually one – the core vocation – will predominate, but the pattern shifts and changes as the circumstances of life change.
- You can never sit back and say to yourself, 'I have found my vocation, now I need give it no more thought.' If you do, you may find yourself blown off course. Vocation is like

an anchor in your life in some respects, but in others it is like a precarious voyage through uncharted waters.

- An avocation is more than a hobby or pastime and less than a vocation. If you are so minded, pursue your avocation as well as your vocation. Advancing on a broad front is a credible military strategy. You may concentrate forces here or there for a time.

- Often, to your surprise, interests or abilities which seemed irrelevant may prove to be highly relevant at some future stage in your life. Like a careful dressmaker or housewife, God seldom wastes the off-cuts or the scraps.

- 'Our nature consists of motion,' wrote Blaise Pascal; 'perfect repose is death.' Vocation strengthens the feeling that life is a journey or pilgrimage.

- Think of yourself as creating your own vocation as much as finding it. Use the raw materials you have received from nature and nurture to fashion the best contribution you can make to life balancing realism about your abilities with an artist's vision of what you have it in you to become.

I am persuaded that every being has their part to play in earth: to be exact, their own part which resembles no other.

André Gide

Checklist – Are You Thinking Creatively?

Would you describe yourself as flexible in implementing your general plans? Can you give two instances?

How did you get on with the Nine Dots and Matchsticks problems?

Are you good at thinking 'outside the box' when it comes to occupational choices?

Has anyone described you as creative and willing take calculated risks in your career?

Do you think that now, having reflected on this chapter, you will be able to fulfil your present role or position in a more creative way?

Are you doing something in the present to help create an expanding future?

Have you ever identified and responded to new needs for services or products caused by change?

Do you welcome the kaleidoscope of change because it brings new opportunities and challenges to your creative spirit?

6

Career or Family?

When first we met we did not guess
That love would prove so hard a master

Robert Bridges

The year, the century, and the millennium turn on the hinge of 1 January 2000, the day I write this chapter. Looking back, what has the twentieth century brought to women? One answer to that question is a single word: *choice*.

In earlier centuries vocation was seen as an essentially male phenomenon. Women, in general, did not pursue careers. Slowly but surely, the doors of almost all professions, careers and trades have been opened to women. Equal opportunity is now the principle we work upon.

That doesn't mean to say that universally all boys and girls are free to choose their vocation according to the principles in this book. If you live in a society where there is only one job available to you – probably inherited from your father – then you are grateful for it and there isn't much room for choice. Yet how many more young men – and women – throughout the world enjoy the privilege (or is it a natural right?) to choose for themselves, and choice brings with it the opportunity to seek and find their own vocation. The growth of choice means that girls have options. They can choose virtually any career they want, if they have the education and training to do it, and pursue it either in place of marriage or in addition to it.

Many women choose motherhood *and* career. That brings with it the ever more pressing problem of reconciling a full-time career with family life.

Men are Procrustean, Women are Holistic

When it comes to vocation, there is a general (male) assumption that men and women think and feel alike about it. But I question if this is the case. Professor Henry Higgins summed up the male attitude in the song in the musical *My Fair Lady*: 'Why can't a women be more like a man?'

A senior city banker, claiming unfair dismissal, described how her (woman) managing director telephoned her with questions about uncompleted work four hours after she had given birth prematurely. She claimed that family commitments meant she could not work the fourteen-hour days the bank expected of her. She was told by the company's personnel manager (another woman) that her interest in seeing her children was akin to someone 'wishing to play squash'.

On one occasion she was reprimanded for missing a training session when her son was taken to hospital with suspected meningitis. 'I was asked why I had not returned immediately,' she said. During her fourth pregnancy she was made redundant and asked to leave the building immediately.

This story, assuming it to be true, suggests to me that the two female managers mentioned had taken on what might pejoratively be called masculine attitudes to work. The narrow focus is on objectives achieved and business results: all that falls outside this tunnel of vision is irrelevant.

When you *focus* on something the surroundings are intentionally blurred to avoid distraction. Such isolation – the hunter selecting one animal in the herd to attack – is a prelude to action. The deployment of resources on a narrow front or upon a specified, identified target is likely to increase effectiveness.

I have noticed that this tunnel vision or narrow focus on to specific, tangible objectives or goals is often advocated in books on careers by men. There may be an unconscious male assumption here that this is the *only* way to achieve success. Moreover, men are procrustean. They tend to disregard or chop off all that doesn't fit into their goal-driven plans.

In Greek legend Procrustes was a robber in Attica who placed all who fell into his hands upon an iron bed. If they were longer than the bed he cut off the overlapping limbs; if shorter he stretched them until they fitted. He was eventually slain by Theseus.

Women are not made for this male Procrustean Bed. They are, I suggest, more holistic about vocation than men. *Holistic* was a word introduced into the English language in 1927 by the South African soldier and statesman Jan Smuts. A keen student of agriculture and the earth sciences, Smuts noted that nature works with wholes. A baby, for example, is not assembled like a kit: it starts as a tiny fertilized seed and *grows* into you or me. I have emphasized *grows* because the concept of growth is important to holistically minded people. Smuts called this tendency in nature *holism*, from the Greek word for 'whole'.

Marion Milner, a psychoanalyst and author, has given us an insight into this arguably innate feminine holism. The child of a distinguished scientific family, she became a researcher in education and industrial psychology, married Dennis Milner, an engineer and inventor, and had one son. Through all this time she was both happy and yet also spiritually unsettled, and she took to writing an intensely self-questioning diary. In 1932 she turned this into a book, *A Life of One's Own*, published under the pseudonym of Joanna Field. Enthusiastically reviewed, it struck a chord with many people, and was reprinted several times. In it she had set herself to grapple with the feeling of being dissatisfied and uncertain about where to go in life. In the context of its time, it was a pioneering piece of work. In her preface she wrote:

> I had assumed that the only desirable way to live was a male way, I had tried to live a male life of objective under-standing and achievement. Always, however, I had felt this was not what really mattered to me. I began to discover impulses towards a different attitude, impulses which eventually led me to find out something of the meaning of

psychic femininity. Thus part of my enterprise was concerned with the discovery that sex was far more than a
physiological matter, though the more fully I understood
this the more important also did the physiological side
become.

Unusually, perhaps, for a psychoanalyst, in her professional
life Marion Milner was willing to draw heavily and openly on
her own inner experience. Firmly rooted as it was in her
humble, humorous, enquiring personality, her writing was
always incisive. Here, in a key passage:

I had been continually exhorted to define my purpose in
life, but I was now beginning to doubt whether life might
be too complex a thing to be kept within the bounds of a
single formulated purpose, whether it would not burst its
way out, or if the purpose were too strong, perhaps grow
distorted like an oak whose trunk had been encircled with
an iron band. I began to guess that my self's need was for
equilibrium, for sun, but not too much, for rain, but not
always. I felt that it was as easily surfeited with one kind
of experience as the body with one kind of food, and that
it had a wisdom of its own, if only I could interpret it. So
I began to have an idea of my life, *not as the slow shaping
of achievement to fit my preconceived purposes, but as the
gradual discovery and growth of a purpose which I did not
know.* I wrote: 'It will mean walking in a fog for a bit, but
it's the only way which is not a presumption, forcing the
self into a theory.'

Marion Milner contrasted her merging and tentative conclusion with the handbooks which told her to define the chief
goal and the subordinate objectives of her life. But introspec-
tion revealed that her mind was always wandering. It took
time for her to accept this tendency, 'but I had at least begun
to guess that my greatest need might be to let go and be free
from the drive after achievement – if only I dared. Then I might

be free to become aware of some other purpose that was more fundamental . . . something which grew out of the essence of one's own nature.'

This explanation by Marion Milner underlines, I believe, the value of distinguishing *purpose* and *goal* or *objective*. Purpose is much broader. She may be right in thinking that the equation of purpose with a long-term goal is a characteristically male tendency. Certainly she would not have subscribed to the advice of Norman Vincent Peale in *Courage and Confidence* (1970):

> To experience the satisfaction and enjoyment of success in life, a definitive goal is essential. Many people fail at this vital point. The goal must be definite and specific, not in any sense vague or fuzzy. And to prove attainable, its image needs to be sharpened and re-sharpened continually, so that it stands out vividly in your thoughts. You must know, at all times, precisely and for certain what it is you want to accomplish and achieve. Strong and organised purpose-fulness towards a definite objective will focus your powers into a strong motivation in attainment of your goal.

The distinction between *purpose*, or a sense of purpose on the one hand and more tangible *aims* or *goals* on the other has not escaped some perceptive male authors, however. Writing in 1912 in his *Note Books*, Samuel Butler said: 'A man should have any number of little aims about which he should be con-scious and for which he should have names, but he should have neither name for, nor consciousness concerning, the main aim [purpose] of his life.'

> *Haunting the lucidities of life*
> *That are my daily beauty, moves a theme*
> *Beating along my undiscovered mind.*
>
> John Drinkwater, 'The Wood', in *Loyalties*

Marion Milner set out to explore that 'undiscovered mind'. She suggests to us that the unknown, purposeful 'theme' is not only broad but deep: it wells up like a spring from the depths of our being.

Tending to live more closely to the springs of their being than men do – if one can ever generalize about such matters – women are much less likely to invest all their time and energies into achievement as narrowly conceived. Their sense of vocation tends to be holistic. It is wide-angle rather than narrow-focus. It embraces a web of relationships of which job or career and its sub-set of relationships are usually a part, not to be equated with the whole. Its natural centre is the family, but it extends much wider than that.

Vocation is in one important sense a synonym for creation. In Genesis, God *calls* into existence: his voice or word is depicted as the agent of creation. 'God said, "Let there be light," and there was light.' To bear children is a strong natural imperative for most women; it is their natural vocation, what they feel drawn or created to do. It is fundamental. But how can bearing children and caring for them be reconciled with having a full-time career? What does that 'theme beating along my undiscovered mind' have to say to me about that dilemma?

The Case of the Company President

At thirty-four Penny Hughes was president of Coca-Cola in Britain and destined for an even greater role in its global empire, but she turned her back on her job to take on an even bigger challenge – motherhood. Five years later, in a *Daily Mail* interview (10 November 1999), she reviewed the choice she had made.

'The leadership position I had was very demanding,' she said. She continued:

> I just knew that I couldn't, in all honesty, do the job as well as I wished to, bring up a young family, have a marriage and have some time to myself. I just didn't think that mix was possible.
>
> I always thought I could do what I call the brain part of

the job, of running Coca-Cola here in the UK, make the strategic decisions, lead the business in that way, but the managerial part, the inspiring leadership, really requires emotion and I suppose that's what I wanted to put into the family and I just knew I couldn't mix the two. You only get it once. By the time I had my first boy, Alex, I was thirty-five. I had on purpose kept going with my career another couple of years in order to reach my potential. I suppose my husband and I put off having a family until I had reached that stage.

Once you decide you want a family, you want to spend time with them. The choice for me was very simple. I just knew that to run that job and to have a family was just going to stretch me too far.

Mrs Hughes combines child-raising with several part-time business interests which she conducts from the terrace home in Twickenham, south-west London, that she shares with her computer analyst husband.

I'm a broader, deeper person and I've learned things about myself that are good and bad that I wouldn't have done. I always knew that I'm quick with my brain and you can't always be like that with children. You've got to be much more patient and teach them slowly and remember that they are not always rational. What I put into the children uses my emotional and managerial skills and sometimes I have to turn those up a bit. The children are often more pestering than any of the people I worked with at Coca-Cola.

Of her decision to become a full-time mother, rather than make use of crèches or childminders to try to 'have it all' like the investment banker Nicola Horlick, Mrs Hughes said:

My perspective is that I made it for myself and my close family. They are the only people who really mattered. It is such a difficult decision for women and, I think, for men too. It was right for me, it may not be right for others. For me, it was an easy way out. I could have continued to do well at Coca-Cola, but the children come first. If they have to go to the doctor or to school, their needs always come first. You can't have those days again. It was for me as much as for them. I am under no illusion about how lucky I am. For many women the choice isn't there. They have to work and bring up children.

Her own childhood also had a major influence on the decision to quit corporate life. 'I know how happy my childhood was and how important education was,' she said.

You've only got relatively few years to help someone. Eighteen years and they are gone, so you have only got that time to help them develop their potential. That's all you can do. My husband has become a dad too so he has had his gripes. He works from home, so we see a lot more of each other than we did before and that's something I wanted.

Although her career is on hold, and will stay so at least until her sons are at school, it appears that you can't keep a good businesswoman down. 'I still get an enormous amount out of my business responsibilities and I have to say I'm a better businesswoman than I am a mother,' said Penny Hughes. 'Business comes so easily to me as opposed to motherhood which is so challenging.'

The story of Penny Hughes illustrates just how very *personal* are the choices made in response to the dilemma facing millions of women – family or career. There are no right or wrong solutions; every situation is unique. As I said, women have the advantage – as Penny Hughes reveals – of living closer to their inner compass than men.

Using the analogy of vocation and avocation that I explored in the last chapter, what Penny is doing is exchanging one for the other. Her latent vocation as a mother moves centre stage with the birth of her two sons; her vocation as a business leader steps back into the wings. But she feeds or keeps alive her interests and skills in business by part-time work. She doesn't plan the future, but she is maintaining her capacity – her option – of returning full-time to business.

Exercise

Penny Hughes sacrificed a salary of £250,000 a year. Make a list of five rewards which finding and following her vocation have so far brought her.

The Case of the Eminent Sculptor

Dame Elizabeth Frink achieved fame as a sculptor. Yet she combined her vocation as an artist with her vocation as wife and mother. She had several advantages: work could be done at home and there was money to employ domestic help.

When living in Dorset, for example, with her third husband, farmer and racehorse trainer Alex Csáky, together with both their respective mothers and the children of previous marriages living nearby, she employed a cook-housekeeper. But her son Lin remembered that throughout his childhood his mother was the person who did all the cooking and housework. Despite her feminist beliefs Dame Elizabeth always perceived the management of the household to be her responsibility.

'A woman artist who doesn't want children, husbands, lovers or whatever can go off and be as single-minded and independent as a man,' she said. 'Otherwise women are stuck with the millstone of domestic responsibility. It's what you choose.'

It's what you choose. Freedom of choice is the key. The nature of your talents or gifts is clearly a factor. It is easier to be a novelist, artist or sculptor, or pursue vocations where much can be done on computers, and also manage a household, than be a surgeon or an opera singer on the global circuit. We all have to make judgements and even compromises, though the art of being flexible takes you a long way.

Another key factor is your partner and his/her attitudes. Indeed one way of looking at marriage is to see it as a vocational partnership.

Marriage as a Vocation Partnership

The model of marriage where the woman bears the children, runs the family and administers the home – *her* natural vocation – while the man goes out to work and pursues *his* vocation, is certainly common, but it is not the only one. The natural epicentre of a woman's shifting network of valuable relationships is the core family – parents, husband, children, grandchildren. But a woman who *only* lives for her children is arguably falling short of her vocation as a woman.

That, in parenthesis, brings me to a defence of marriage. I am aware that it may sound a bit dated to talk about marriage when so many people are living happily with partners of the opposite or same sex. It is true that women (usually) urge their partners to convert the arrangement into marriage when children arrive or perhaps – often much less effectively it seems – when they feel insecure about the relationship.

My argument for marriage would be on different grounds. Unlike informal or unwed partnerships, marriage is a public affair. It announces a new cell in the body of society. It gives a woman a firm base from which to fulfil her wide-angle vocation for people and relationships *for the good of society*.

One natural way of doing that – a self-effacing one admittedly – is through the practical support and help a wife gives to her husband: *his* vocation becomes *their* vocation. For example, the Egyptologist Jack Plumley's first wife Gwen entered into the spirit of his work, in spite of having three sons to look after.

As *The Times* obituary of her husband records, 'she became the quartermaster of the Egyptian expeditions, piling up food for the team for three months, and making drawings of the finds. She published a diary of one of the expeditions, and a little study of the tambur or Sudanese lyre.'

Gwen Plumley was not less vocational than her husband, but her vocation was different and complementary. It included working with him as a helpmate, but also her wider calling as wife and mother. I bet she made endless cups of tea for the parishioners!

That wider social role of kindness and friendship – a quilt-work of small and unremembered acts to neighbours and others outside the family – is as much vocational as painting pictures or writing books. Often, however, this work of love goes on without a word of appreciation, and that can test a woman's spirit: for praise or recognition by those who know us best is the oxygen of the human spirit.

In my course as an author I have written two biographies, both of Puritan English gentlemen who became political and military leaders in the Civil War during the seventeenth century. Both men lost their wives in childbirth, and both wrote epitaphs extolling their virtues. John Hampden's words above Elizabeth's tomb are especially apt in this context because they evoke an image of that wider feminine vocation that I have been trying to capture in words:

> In her pilgrimage,
> The stay and comfort of her neighbours,
> The love and glory of a well ordered family,
> The delight and happiness of tender parents –
> But a crown of blessings to a husband.
> In a wife, to all an eternal pattern of goodness
> And cause of love, while she was
> In her dissolution a loss invaluable to each . . .

It is equally true that where a wife is pursing a vocation outside the home her husband can share in it, even if only by providing practical support and a listening ear. Teamwork is valuable, and not only because of professional and technical synergy, the complementary jigsaw of skills. Teams give their individual members emotional and moral support. Two heads are better than one – and so are two spirits working in harness and in harmony.

Tensions between roles will arise in most modern marriages, as the two partners change and develop. But if the relationship is a strong one – if the partners love each other – 'role negotiation' can take place. That's just a grand phrase for creative compromise, for working out together a mutually advantageous solution.

Primary and Secondary Roles

In the last chapter I explored the idea that we can have vocations and avocations. Sometimes we can pursue them in tandem. Sometimes one is pursued, then the other replaces it – like runners in a relay race. It may make sense for both men and women to think of their lives in terms of vocation and avocation. Under which of those two headings 'marriage' and 'work' fall in any phase of your life will depend upon your circumstances.

With a young family, there is greatest support for a model that gives women primary but not sole responsibility for the children, and men primary but not sole responsibility for breadwinning. This concept of primary and secondary responsibilities ties in well with the more holistic sense of vocation in women.

The Integrating Purpose

'I always wanted both a career and a family, and tried to integrate them, but I have never found an integrating purpose,' writes the woman novelist A. S. Byatt.

Perhaps, in the light of Marion Milner and Samuel Butler, we might say that it's not so much a question of not *finding* a purpose with that capability as of recognizing that it's there already and *naming* it.

There is, however, quite a strong case for leaving that purpose without a name, like that altar that St Paul found in

Athens dedicated to AN UNKNOWN GOD. Yet if you assume (see p. 41) that our *aims* should relate to our *purpose*, it stands to reason that if there appears to be a conflict between two *aims* – say between career or family? – we should appeal to the next level up, so to speak, for a settlement. A university, for example, may have *teaching* and *research* as its two principal aims, but these are difficult to reconcile unless there is a more general and integrating purpose formulated, such as 'the promotion of *learning*'.

Such statements of purpose only do their work if these are understood as concepts rather than definitions, for it's their function to be broad and encompassing. Yet a purpose does need *some* definition, which implies some sort of naming, otherwise it can hardly function at all as an arbiter or as a navigational aid in life's journey.

> *In the deserts of the heart*
> *Let the healing fountain start . . .*
>
> W. H. Auden

Yes, the purpose of our lives remains without a name. Whoever discovers *that* will have made the greatest discovery of all time. Yet it may be that there is a clue given to us – *love*. Still, I use even that word – *any* word – with much hesitation. Apart from its confusing overtones, to try to see the purpose of your life *love* might sound decidedly pretentious. Not that you need to go public on the subject. Nor is it necessary to judge yourself, or invite others to do so, against the measure of love. None of us would pass all its tests.

Why do I suggest *love* as our one essential clue to that inner holistic or integrating spiritual purpose of life? In this context, because it is arguably the highest common denominator in both marriage and family life on the one hand and vocation on the other. It is not necessary to defend that assertion in relation to marriage – who would deny that love is its soul? – but it is less clear that love is present in vocation.

Yet, as we have seen above the word *love* crops up in relation to vocation (as opposed to career, profession or trade). Vocational people speak of *loving* their work. Even if they do not actually use that word the way they act and talk suggests it. They also love *through* their work – God or humankind, or both. Again, they may prefer more neutral words like *serving others* or *doing good* or *making a contribution*, but that amounts in one way or another to 'loving your neighbour'. (To love one's neighbour doesn't mean that you necessarily have to *like* them: it means to will their good and take what steps you can to realize it.) Love is the descant, the grace-notes over the music of vocation. Tolstoy wrote in *The Resurrection*:

> Men think there are circumstances when they may treat their fellow beings without love, but no such circumstances exist. Inanimate objects may be dealt with without love ... but human beings cannot be treated without love ... If you feel no love for men – leave them alone. Occupy yourself with things, with your own self, with anything you please, but not with men.

Why do so many women gravitate towards jobs that involve caring, teaching or serving others, especially the needy? Partly, it must be admitted, because they are often easier to combine with a mother's primary role of childcare. But also because, quite unselfconsciously, they catch the light of an unspoken, unknown, inner purpose. As the proverb says: *The soul of woman lives in love*.

Summary of Key Points

- Career or family? This dilemma faces millions of women – and men, too. It is more pressing for women because motherhood is at the epicentre of their natural vocation. And the deeply ingrained pattern of complementary father/mother responsibilities is persistent.
- Choice is a necessary condition for vocation. If you have no choice – like a man having only one job on offer or none,

or like a woman with marriage as her only option – you may be lucky, it may turn out to be your vocation. But if you can freely choose the work you want to do, or the state of life – single or married – you want to be in, then you are much more likely to experience whatever you choose as your vocation.

- Vocation may be experienced differently by a woman than a man, and if so that would be an important discovery. Here I have suggested that for women it is more holistic, more diffuse and more centred on a web of personal relationships. The male model – the tendency to equate purpose with sharply-defined goals and objectives – is not the only one. In fact, it is an unwise confusion for men as well as women.

- Vocation for a woman is not necessarily 'found' as if by a masculine-type hunt, nor 'conquered' by an elaborate siege. It unfolds gradually, especially for women, who, perhaps through living closer to their inner being, are better than men at 'listening with the third ear', or sensing where their inner compass is directing them.

- Career or family? There is no right or wrong choice. You can have one or the other. Or you can attempt to eat your cake and have it, as most of us do. We need to make the choices with our partners, taking their interests into account as seriously as we take our own. Beware, however, of the compromise that you may live to regret.

- Love is the integrating purpose which alone has power to bind together our several vocations and enable them to move together in one harmony. For, in Ovid's words, 'Love's dominion, like kings', admits to no partition.'

- If love suggests or points to an overarching principle, it doesn't release us from the requirement to work it out – and to rediscover it – in changing circumstances. The author Ursula Le Guin wrote: 'Love doesn't sit here like a stone; it is to be made like bread, remade all the time, made new.'

> *I tell thee Love is Nature's second sun,*
> *Causing a spring of virtues when he shines.*
>
> George Chapman

Checklist – Career or Family?

'Women who stay at home to look after their families do not have a vocation.' Do you agree?

Have you considered – and discussed with your partner – whether or not you wish to combine your vocation as a wife and mother with an avocation – a career?

If so, have you together worked out a balance between primary and secondary roles to accommodate both bread-winning and childbearing?

Are there any circumstances in which you would put your career before the interests of your family?

Can you think of two women who harmoniously combine work using their natural talents with caring for a family?

And two men?

Can you think of a better concept than love to integrate your vocation at work and in the family?

7

Corporate Vocations

What is the city but the people?

William Shakespeare, *Coriolanus*

One common assumption – usually unconscious – is that vocation is an individual matter. The idea that a group or an organization might have a vocation is alien to us, yet the Bible depicts God as calling Israel, a confederation of twelve desert tribes: 'When Israel was a child, I loved him, and out of Egypt I called my son' (Hosea 1:11).

Of course in earlier times individuality was much less pronounced: people felt themselves to be first and foremost members of a tribe – a corporate personality with its own god – and only secondarily as individual persons. Israelites, whatever their individual thoughts in the matter, shared in the corporate vocation of Israel, like those who inherit stock in a modern company. A *member* is literally a bodily part or function. Membership of the tribe is organic; if one member suffers, all suffer. All for one; one for all.

That same sense of corporate vocation animated the first members of the Christian Church. St Paul used the analogy of the human *body*, with each function – apostles, prophets, teachers, leaders, helpers, administrators – as a complementary member of the whole body (1 Corinthians 12:14–31).

Later, the monasteries and convents emerged as *communities* of men and women called to realize on earth the ideals of the Kingdom of God. To do that they set themselves apart as far as possible from the contaminations of 'the world, the flesh and the devil'. As rules and structures developed, they became organizations – international ones in the case of the larger orders.

An individual might then, as now, have a strong inner urge – from God or as if from God – to become a monk or nun. Such an inward vocation or calling was regarded as a prerequisite for such a demanding live. (Oddly enough, it was not a condition for becoming a priest. The priests of Israel were born into the priestly tribe. St Augustine was almost forced against his will into being ordained and consecrated bishop by the Christians in Hippo. Thanks to the reformer Martin Bucer, the requirement for an inner vocation associated with monks and nuns was introduced into the *Book of Common Prayer*'s ordination service: 'Do you trust that you are inwardly moved by the Holy Spirit to take upon you this office of deacon?')

If you didn't have a vocation to be a monk, you could still join the vocational community as a lay brother. In the larger monasteries the monks could not have maintained their daily round of worship, study and labour without the help of the lay brothers.

It looks so far as if the concept of corporate vocation – communities of vocational people and their supporters or auxiliaries – is confined to religion. But it soon burst those bounds with, for example, the rise of universities, a name that derives from the Latin *universitas*, the whole, and which later came to mean a society, guild or corporation. Universities were originally a corporation of teachers and students formed for the purpose of giving and receiving instruction in a limited range of subjects at a higher level than that provided at school. The hospital also developed in a similar way as a vocational community. But the idea that *business* organizations – banks, companies, commercial enterprises – as well as monasteries or schools, universities or hospitals, can be seen as and developed into vocational communities is potentially a quantum leap of the imagination, and yet I believe that this is what is needed today.

Modern Organisations as Vocational Communities

Business strategy theorists can make heavy reading. But whilst travelling this improbable road I saw the light!

Let me explain what I mean. There are masses of theories as to how businesses might achieve sustained profitability and avoid being knocked off their perch by competitors. But one theory stood out and hit me. In the jargon it is called *resource-based* strategy. Put in its simplest terms, it means that competitive advantage goes to those companies that identify their unique capabilities and fill their resultant niche. Their produce and service is excellent. Above all, they truly serve the needs of their customers. Where have you heard that before?

What I saw in my flash of illumination is that vocations are not just for individuals. A business organization (in the widest sense of the word) can also have a vocation.

It follows logically that many people who would not see themselves as vocational persons *individually* – in the sense that an artist, poet or inventor might – now have an immense opportunity to find their vocations as members of a team, in an organization or community which is pursuing a vocational purpose: to use all its natural interests, talents or abilities in the service of others or the common good.

The concept of organizations as vocational persons writ large is so new and unfamiliar – a paradox in fact – that it is worth exploring further before I come to the practical implications for you as you seek your own vocation in life.

Here I must acknowledge a debt to Professor Dorothy Emmet, a philosopher still writing books in her nineties – that's vocation! Her book *Function, Purpose and Powers* (1958) was seminal to my own thought about vocation in organisations, as you will see.

The Five Hallmarks of a Vocational Business

At this point you are probably wishing you could tell me something along these lines: 'I wish that what you say was true,

John. But the organization I work for is anything but vocational. It has no altruism; the bottom line is all that matters.
It treats its customers with, shall we say, indifference – and its
staff worse than that. It trades on yesterday's products and
services. Our senior managers have no talent for leadership in
any direction, let alone forwards. It's a question of one damn
thing after another. The fun went out of it for me after the
second lot of redundancies – the fifth lot go next month. I hope
it's my turn next. Early retirement would be better than this.
How can you say so confidently that you have seen the future,
and it is the vocational organization?'

My answer to that question is simple. Evolution – the sur-
vival of the fittest – favours businesses that are transforming
themselves into vocational communities. Like the fabulous
phoenix bird, they are reinventing themselves on vocational
lines. Paradox it may be, but only those businesses that are
vocational will enjoy sustained success. They will exemplify
the following five hallmarks:

1 *Customer Focus* The classic end of business is maximizing
shareholder wealth. The vocational company doesn't think
like that. It puts service to its customers and to society first,
and it ensures that its products and services are of a quality
and price to meet the customer's needs. If it does that successfully the shareholders will have a fair return for their
investment.

2 *Niches* The exploration of business strategy leads us to see
success as knowing and using one's unique resources in
relation to the market place. It is in the individuality or even
uniqueness of these assets – especially people and intellectual
capital – that competitive advantage lies.

3 *Creativity* Change calls for new ideas and new ways of working. New products and services are needed. Creative individuals may supply ideas, but it takes creative teamwork to
innovate – to bring the product or service to market.

4 *Leadership* As companies become more vocational, leading
creative teams and organizations calls for vocational leaders
rather than old-style 'command and control' managers.

5 *Enjoyment* Despite the competitive pressures and ever more demanding challenges those who work for vocational companies enjoy their work and especially working as a team with their colleagues. *No one does a job well unless they love to do it.*

In the context of such organizations we can discover that being a manager, for example, is a vocation as much as being a doctor, teacher or musician. A manager helps to bring order out of chaos. By serving the organization he or she serves also the community. Or, putting it more accurately, a vocational person can transform their work in an organisation, such as being a manager, into a vocation.

Tomorrow's People

Those who work in tomorrow's vocational organizations will need both individual and general characteristics and skills.

You will have noticed that both *service* and *creativity* feature prominently on the above profile of the successful company. The need for quality of service to the customer – the need to create a satisfied customer – has become commonplace, even a cliché, in business philosophy. The problem is how to achieve it. Endless 'customer service' training programmes don't seem to do the trick. The problem lies much deeper, in the beliefs, values and attitudes of those involved in the enterprise.

Too often, for example, service is seen as literally servile – something beneath one's dignity. As I have already said, the word service comes from the Latin *servus*, a slave. To be 'in service' was historically to be at the lowest end of the social spectrum. Unless, that is, one happened to be serving the king or queen. Then the high status of the monarch lent status to the royal servants or 'ministers'. 'The customer is king' remains a business cliché until you see the king in the customer.

In each of us there is a king. Speak to him And he will come forth.

Scandinavian proverb

For vocational people service is not a problem: it is a central part of the purpose of their lives. They have that necessary vision that does see the value of each person whose needs they have the privilege of meeting. Money or a high salary is an extra reward, one usually made necessary by having to earn a living in a money economy. But the true reward lies in the opportunity of being able to use your talents to the full in the service of others, and so fulfilling the aim of your working life.

When Queen Elizabeth I thanked her chief minister Lord Burghley at the close of his many years of service to her and the nation, he replied: '*My service has been but a price of my duty, and my vocation has been too great a reward.*'

Vocation is Alive and Well

Richard Morrison wrote an article in *The Times* (4 January 2000) in which he describes how a serious accident – he was knocked off his cycle by a motorist – changed the way he viewed life. He was immensely struck by the kindness of the professionals he encountered, as well as others – the public and his neighbours. Some patients and relatives repaid this kindness with ingratitude, but Morrison had seen a new, life-transforming vision of the greatness in human nature waiting to be released by genuine need:

> So, four months on, with my new titanium-enriched ankle creaking back to life, what have I learnt? It is this: if you are lucky in life, if you have never needed to lean on other people, you never become aware of the abundant wells of kindness in this world. Before the accident I was in that position. In fact, I was more cynical than that. I imagined that modern Britain was a pretty hardhearted place, bristling with 'me first' selfishness.
>
> Now I know differently. First, I have seen for myself what 'vocation' means. Throughout Britain there must

be thousands of nurses like the ones who selflessly scurried round my ward. And not just nurses. The concept of 'duty' is alive and well throughout the emergency services, and in teaching and voluntary work, too. The fact that society takes advantage of such dedication by paying peanuts is a stain on the fabric of modern Britain. So is the fact that such lion hearts are often battling against overwhelming bureaucratic odds to keep our public services from collapse.

But even more touching has been the compassion of those who are not paid to be kind: friends and strangers alike. And this has wrought a change in me. Modern life is often frenetic and brutish. It is easy to lapse into the belief that if you don't trust anybody except yourself, you won't be disappointed. But if you don't give people a chance to show nobility and compassion, you will never know that these qualities exist.

They do, in bucketfuls, even in the supposedly uncaring non-communities of modern London. It took a bad road accident to reveal that to me. But I carry the thought into 2000, and hope that I am not too often disillusioned.

Can business attract vocational people – those committed to using their talents for the common good? Too often nowadays the sole end of business appears to be money-making, not service. In fact, as I have said, money-making and the production of goods and services that people need are indissolubly linked. And we now know that sustained profitable success in business – paradoxically – only goes to those companies that know and fulfil their vocations as business organizations. That means creating delighted customers.

Alongside *service* in vocation there sits *creativity*. Creative people tend to be vocational, and vocational people tend to become creative.

New ideas – the seeds of either new products and services

or significant incremental improvements in present ones – arise in the minds of individuals. So if you want creativity in your organization you must find and retain those who are vocationally tuned to the work you are doing.

I make a distinction between creativity and innovation. Creativity is having the new ideas; innovation is getting them to market in the shape of new products and services. If the source of new ideas is in the creative imagination of a talented individual, innovation always requires teamwork. Some of the roles required in such teams are not what you would normally call vocational, but in fact they are. A person in such a role becomes vocational by virtue of being part of a vocational team.

Like any vocational community some members of a business enterprise will be more vocational than others. Even if you are not one of the main vocational players – if you are a hospital porter or cleaner rather than a doctor or nurse, for example – you can fulfil such a role with a creative spirit, not just to earn money. Your role in an organization, however humble it may be, is the raw material of *your* vocation as a member of a vocational team. You may not have a vocation in the individual sense, but you have found your vocation: it is your *share* in a corporate vocation.

Vocation and Role

This concept of role is a key to understanding teams and organizations. From Shakespeare onwards, this theatrical term has been a key metaphor for the part played by a person in society or life.

A *role* in this social sense is more than occupying a position or office. A role consists of the expectations that people have of what someone in that job will do, irrespective of who that person is. For example, we have certain expectations of how a police officer or doctor will behave towards a member of the public or a patient. If they act outside their role we find it disconcerting, to say the least. Conformity to a role affords predictability, but it also imposes constraints.

Role as expectations works both ways. A good patient, for example, wants to get better and does what they agree to do with the doctor towards that end. Of course it is possible for either party to have *unrealistic* expectations. Satisfaction varies directly with what you get and inversely with what you expect. So if you reduce your expectations to zero, you are unlikely to be disappointed. People often adapt in this way to situations where roles are performed poorly, rather than trying to make them better.

In a team or organization, then, you occupy a role or function which is complementary to others *in the light of a common task*. 'Function' describes the action for which a person or thing is specially fitted or used for, or for which it exists. As the special kind of activity proper to a person, the mode of action by which he or she fulfils their purpose, it is very close in meaning to what I have been describing as vocation. What is the difference?

Vocation Versus Bureaucracy

'Such lion hearts are often battling against overwhelming bureaucratic odds,' said Richard Morrison in Box 7.1. Vocational people in organizations often see themselves as in a state of war with the administrators – now more universally known as the management. Equally, administrators or managers find vocational people hard to control. It can become like Milton's picture of an unhappy marriage in *Paradise Lose*:

> Thus they in mutual accusation spent,
> The fruitless hours, but neither self-condemning.

As organizations grow in vocational stature this civil 'war without an enemy' will be seen as a thing of the past. As long ago as 1958, Dorothy Emmet pointed the way forward in *Function, Purpose and Powers*:

> If vocational people work from some inner incentive proper to themselves, they will tend to be, or rather perhaps to

become, strong characters. They will need to develop considerable powers of concentration, and the ability to go on in spite of discouragements. In so far as their work can also be looked on as role behaviour (and from the point of view of one kind of social analysis all work is this), they will be likely to perform their roles in ways individual to themselves . . .

How original a person dares be in carrying out a role may largely depend on how strong a character he is. How far he can go and still be tolerated rather than ostracised as a 'deviant' will depend on the attitude of other people in society to their strong characters, and how much concern they have for encouraging possibilities of vocation. *This is where wisdom and imagination are called for from administrators, and where indeed administration itself calls for vocational qualities.* Those who stress the potentially anarchic side of vocational people do not always see the vocational quality present in some administrators. This is because administrators are largely concerned with maintaining a social group or organisation according to recognised norms. They are concerned with seeing that departures from recognised procedures do not pass beyond certain limits, and thus they will be likely to set a primary value on stability, and very properly, since they have responsibility for seeing that the organisation is maintained and survives as a going concern. Every organisation thus tends to acquire a conservative functional momentum.

The sentence I have placed in italics above contains the nub of the matter. Management or administration is a complementary vocation. Or, to put it another way, if those performing the more 'maintenance' functions of administration do so as their vocations, then the organization will not lapse into mere bureaucracy, a system marked by officialism, red tape and the proliferation of official routine.

To summarize: as an organization grows in its vocation the ancient division between first-hand contributors and administrative staff is transcended. The primary role of the former is to practise their vocation, but they have a secondary role as managers or administrators, even if only of themselves. The latter, in turn, develop an understanding and rapport with their vocational colleagues: for them management or administration is a vocation that calls for their creativity as well as their professional skills.

In some respects vocational organizations may appear to the outsider to be rather ramshackle, like sprawling farm buildings. They are loosely constructed and seem about to collapse! But they give people that essential freedom with the limits of their roles which they need to do their work creatively, so that it becomes an expression of their inner values and spirit and not just a competent performance.

Yet, because the administrative and financial people in the team are also fulfilling their vocations – both as professionals and also as team members – then this 'ramshackle' organization will be both efficient and effective. A steely self-discipline will rest below the surface of creative informality and enjoyment.

May I add a 'health warning'? If your organization drops down to the level of mediocrity, then you must expect the vocational people in it to move on to 'pastures new'.

Lastly, the vocational community of today and tomorrow – employing men and women in more-or-less equal numbers across the organizational spectrum – will pay far more than the present customary lip service to *family-friendly* policies. It will be, for example, the enemy of unnecessarily long hours. It will not be rigid or inflexible in allowing people time to care for sick children or elderly parents. Too many employers fail to implement even legislation-related policies, basically because – through lack of good leadership – they don't trust their employees. The vocational organization will take into account the wider vocations of their partners or members, which for men and women alike encompass family as well.

Checklist – Have You Found Your Vocation in a Team?

Before reading this chapter, did you assume that vocation was essentially an *individual* matter, not something that you could share in with others?

Have you experienced and enjoyed working in teams or organizations in a role that is complementary to others?

Great modern innovations and great service organizations call for teamwork. Do you agree?

Do you regard the mechanics who service the aircraft you fly in as vocationally inferior to the pilots in the cockpit?

Can you think of any vocational person working on their own who doesn't depend upon others in order to bring their product to the end-user?

List three organisations which strike you as being already vocational in the sense described in this chapter.

Knowing yourself as you do, do you now consider it more likely than not that you will discover your vocation in a team/organization context, rather than 'going it alone'?

Summary of Key Points

- 'I sat alone,' said the prophet Jeremiah. There is a strong connection between vocation and being an individual. When we think of vocational people, for example, they are often strongly individual. Often they feel as if they have separated – or been separated – from the herd. The artist is a case in point. For the most part, it is solitary work. 'Because it is solitary,' said C. Day Lewis, 'it can tempt him to satanic egotism.'
- Teams and organizations as well as individuals can be vocational. This gives you much more choice. You may find your

vocation as a 'sole proprietor' or more probably you can discover it as a 'member' in a corporate 'body' – a corporate person if you like, but one that can achieve tasks that transcend the capability of any single individual. Committees are notoriously bad at writing poems or painting pictures. But what individual *on their own* built a jet airliner or carried out a heart transplant operation?

- Vocational people tend to become individualists in the sense that they pursue a markedly independent course in thought or action. But it is a mistake to confuse vocation with individualism, or to see a vocational person as *always* working on their own. A family, team organization or community can be vocational as much as an individual.

- The importance of this point for someone seeking their vocation should not be underestimated. Without being aware of it, you may be looking in the wrong place. A 'stand alone' vocation, like being a painter or sculptor, is not what you are after. In fact, vocationally speaking, you are not complete. You need to join up with one or more other people in order to experience and fulfil your vocation.

- As a general principle on this vocational path you surrender some of your independence, but the compensation is *that together we can achieve much more than any single individual on their own.*

- A key concept in organizational life is *role*. The greatest actors are those whose own personality you hardly notice: the sublimate themselves in their role.

- Actually 'the river of life' is taking all organizations forwards to discovering corporate vocation, whether they choose to 'go with the flow' or not. For competitive advantage is acquired by those organizations which exhibit the five vocational hallmarks: customer focus, niches, creativity, leadership and enjoyment.

It takes a whole village to raise a child.

African proverb

8

Serve to Lead

The task of leadership is not to put greatness into people, but to elicit it, for the greatness is there already.

John Buchan

For much of my working life I have thought, written and talked about leadership – it has in fact been fairly central to my own sense of vocation – yet oddly a simple truth about it has eluded me until I came to write this book. *It is vocational people who tend to become leaders.*

There is a second truth about good leaders, too, which is germane to this book. *Leadership is the talent for enabling others to use their talents.* In this chapter I want to explore with you both these facets.

Vocation as the Matrix of Leadership

Putting it slightly differently, leadership is a secondary calling, in the sense of being sequential – it follows on from the first. It's the necessary condition for leadership that you find and live your vocation. That doesn't *guarantee* that you will become a leader. For another necessary condition is that you have some aptitude for leadership. Again, even that doesn't mean that you will certainly become a leader. The sufficient condition lies partly in the situation and partly in the perceptions of the other people involved. Those two factors – the situation and the response of others to you – govern whether or not you will be seen to be – and be accepted as – a leader in your chosen field.

Notice that the sufficient condition here is *not* merely that you are appointed to a managerial position, that is, one that requires leadership at some level of responsibility in an organization. There are thousands of people occupying such positions in enterprises who are not fulfilling the true role of a leader. Role, you recall, is best applicable in terms of expectations. You can be appointed (or elected) a manager or commander, but *you are not a leader until your appointment is ratified in the hearts and minds of those who work for you or with you.*

What is a Leader's General Role?

At its broadest, a leader's role is *to go in front of people and thereby show them the way forward.* Our words 'lead' and 'leader' come from a northern European root meaning a path, road, track, or the course of a ship at sea. These are journey words. To lead is to go ahead, like a guide who knows the path and the dangers or difficulties ahead. But, unlike a guide, a leader needs to be able to take people with them and sometimes even inspire them to make the journey.

How does vocation fit into that picture? People tend to follow those who know where they are going, those with vision and creative imagination. Vocational people are the ones who tend to have those attributes.

Sometimes vocational people are pioneers by accident; they don't expect anyone to follow their lead and are surprised – even annoyed – to find they have company, as the following example illustrates.

Have you ever had that feeling that you would like to get away from it all and retire on your own to a desert island? That urge overcame a young man of twenty called Antony in Egypt around 270AD. He felt called to lead a life that matched the demands of the Kingdom of God in the Gospels. He gave away all his possessions. Then he journeyed to the Egyptian desert and took up residence in a remote cave.

You might rate Antony's leadership prospects pretty low at

this point! But true vocation acts like a magnet. Other young men sold their goods and followed his example, ensconcing themselves around his hermitage. At thirty-five, Antony sought solitude once more by moving further away to a mountain in the desert. But his followers again sought him out, and for twenty years he gave leadership to those drawn to this vocation. He founded the first religious community, one following a rule of life under an elected leader. All monastic life stemmed from Antony's example.

Another solitary who was surprised by leadership was William Wordsworth. He retired to devote himself to poetry in the solitude of his beloved Cumbrian fells and lakes. Yet as a poet he was a pioneer, if not a revolutionary, and other younger poets looked to him as their leader, inspired and encouraged by the trail he blazed. Indeed, when much later one of them, Robert Browning, became convinced that Wordsworth had changed sides and betrayed his theory, he wrote about it in a poem called 'The Lost Leader':

> We that had loved him so, followed him, honoured him,
> Lived in his mild and magnificent eye,
> Learned his great language, caught his clear accents,
> Made him our pattern to live and die.

Exercise

See if you can identify *four* vocational people, two men and two women, who have become leaders as a result of following their vocations.

What is it that people see in such vocational venturers? They see themselves – or the selves they would like to be – writ large. So the first requirement for leadership – be it in the unstructured form I have been describing or in a structured organization – is that *the leader should personify or exemplify the qualities expected or required in their working groups.*

Now it's actually very hard to do that if you are working outside your proper vocational field. If, for example, you can merely play an instrument competently but have no vocation to music, it is very unlikely that you will ever end up in the world's top twenty orchestral conductors!

Some leaders are pioneers in the sense of being among the first in new fields or enterprise. They originate or help to open up a new line of thought or activity or a new method or technical development. In the original military usage, pioneers go ahead to prepare roads for the main body of troops. The pioneers of today are the founders or early workers in a particular field. I have been fortunate to meet many, but one in particular sticks in my mind.

In 1968, when I was Director of Studies at St George's House, it fell to my lot to interview ten or twelve bishops individually, to enlist their support for a new programme for future church leaders which I had begun to plan. The Bishop of Manchester, I recall, met me at the House of Lords and offered as a bonus his six-point programme for the church in our times. One of the items was the care of the dying, not something I had thought about. 'How is that to be done?' I asked. He had no answer.

That evening, when I returned to St George's House, there was a consultation in progress. After dinner I fell into conversation with a tall, bespectacled woman. She told me about her work caring for those with incurable illnesses. It soon became clear to me that she had a vision, she knew what to do. But at that time it was no more than that – a vision. As a result of it and her gift for leadership, the modern hospice movement, as we know it today throughout the world, has largely sprung. Her name was Dr Ciceley Saunders.

Team Leadership

So far we have looked at one side of the coin of leadership – having vision, providing others with direction, going out in front, perhaps without even glancing over your shoulder to see if anyone is following. For that is the way that your inner compass directs you, that's the path for you, even if you tread it alone.

Yet to be a leader, is not the same as to be a pioneer building new roads or scout acting as path-finders ahead of the main body, nor an escort bringing up the rear, nor even a guide whose sole contribution is that they know the way. To lead teams is to take others with you. The other side of the coin of leadership is people-orientated. It is about building teams, creating and fostering teamwork, motivating and inspiring others, establishing trustful communication and developing a climate where each can do something really well.

Clearly, not all vocational people have a natural aptitude for this kind of leadership. The best course for those who don't is probably to concentrate on becoming better in their contribution as specialists. But those vocational people within an organization who do have a talent for leadership – whatever their initial functional specialism happens to be – need to experience something like the reverse thrust of a jet engine: they need to become generalists again. I say *again* because we all start out at school as *generalists* and only gradually do we learn to specialize as we discover our particular talents, interests and aptitudes. So the careers of leaders in organizations can be tracked with the help of a simple model (Figure 8.1).

The shape of a specialist's career, by contrast, would look like an inverted funnel as in Fig. 8.1. In tomorrow's vocational organization, successful specialists will receive the same appreciation, reflected in salary, as leader-manager generalists. What organizations should never do is to promote vocational people who have no talent for leadership in any direction by placing them in charge of others, simply because there isn't any other sanctioned method for rewarding them financially except by making them managers. Not that I mean to suggest that specialists should not be trained in team-working skills. Far from it. If, as I believe, the essence of vocational organiza-

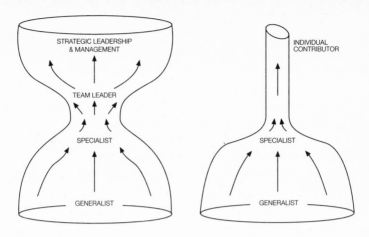

Figure 8.1 The Hourglass-shaped and Invented Funnel Models of Career Change

tions is teamwork, *everyone* – and I do mean everyone – in such a company, enterprise or institution needs to be able to work effectively and in harmony with others.

You will have noticed that I have been distinguishing and naming different levels of leadership responsibility in corporate life, and I must now explain what I mean by these terms. *Team* leaders normally are accountable for about ten people. *Operational* leaders look after a significant part or major function of the business. *Strategic* leaders are at the helm of a whole enterprise. May I remind you that I am using business in its most inclusive sense – enterprise or organizations where people busy themselves to one end or another.

Obviously the aptitude for strategic leadership is much less common than the talent for leading a small team. The core leadership responsibilities – achieving the task, building the team and developing individuals – remain the same at all three levels, but the scale is different. The strategic leader needs more practical intellectual ability. The Greeks called it *phronesis*, which is best rendered 'practical wisdom'. Lawrence of Arabia once called it 'brainy leadership'.

In leadership, as with all vocation, the principle is to *select* (or self-select) according to natural aptitude, and then *develop* that potential. We have the knowledge to do both, but it is not as yet very widely applied. That is one major reason why we have too few organizations that can be described as well led. And that in turn may explain why so few have a sense of corporate vocation.

To summarize: leadership is a symbiotic phenomenon. You will never go out into the street and meet someone who is *just* a leader. They will be a nurse *and* leader, a teacher *and* leader, a salesperson *and* leader, a soldier *and* leader, an administrator or manager *and* leader, and so on. It is the *vocational* nurse, teacher or salesperson who tends to become a leader, because their heart and soul is in the business. They don't lack enthusiasm, for example, that key leadership quality. If they can develop the necessary leadership skills at whatever level they aspire to reach, they will be accepted by their colleagues as natural leaders. Leadership gives them a means of adding extra value.

Nelson may have had epaulettes on his shoulders, but they were not the main source of his authority. *Authority flows to the one who knows.* As he lay dying, Nelson is reported to have said, 'Thank God I have done my duty.' The words sum up the selfless spirit of duty, to the point of self-sacrifice, that animated him. It was the very foundation of his calling – regardless of the vanity which made him human and therefore closer to us.

Thus Nelson exemplifies a principle enunciated by Joseph Conrad in *The Mirror of the Sea*, one that applies to *all* leaders in every field:

The genuine masters of their craft – I say this confidently from my experience of ships – have thought of nothing but of doing their best by the vessel under their charge. To forget one's self, to surrender all personal feelings in the service of that fine art, is the only way for a seaman to the faithful discharge of his trust.

A Genius for Leadership

A genius, as opposed to a gift or talent, for leadership is rare in any culture, but occasionally one in a thousand oysters does yield a near-perfect pearl.

Admiral Lord St Vincent once wrote a letter to Horatio Nelson in which he said: 'I never saw a man in our profession . . . who possessed the magic art of infusing the same spirit into others which inspired their own actions . . . all agree there is but one Nelson.' From such a seasoned and wise superior that is a glowing tribute to his junior, one which reflects credit on both men. Will the same ever be said about you?

On shore, it must be added, Nelson could appear to others extremely vain and egotistical to the point of silliness, a show-off who loved to be famous. He made no impression in any other field but his own.

On the deck of a man o' war, everything was different. Nelson had found his vocation as a sailor at a very early age – he went to sea when he was twelve – and his gift, amounting to genius, for naval leadership at all levels unfolded thereafter. On the poop deck he had no need to impress – everyone soon discovered that he knew what to do and was in command of himself as well as others. Nelson's selfless concern for the service and for his men won him all hearts on board his ship and later his fleet.

That brings me to the title of this chapter, 'Serve to Lead'. It is the motto of the Royal Military Academy Sandhurst, where I spent some nine years as a lecturer in military history, and Adviser in Leadership Training, and so those three simple words are close to my heart.

I suppose that the motto of Sandhurst *can* be interpreted merely to mean that you must learn to obey orders before you are entitled to give them. But that is a bit pedestrian. I prefer to interpret the motto as a signpost, pointing to the truth that leadership is a calling, and that – like all other vocations – its end is service. Leo Tolstoy put it so simply: 'The vocation of men and women is to serve others.'

A Prospector for Talent

Whether or not they receive any financial remuneration for their work all vocational people are paid in the coinage of joy. One of the joyful rewards of leadership is to discern, encourage and release talents in people that they did not suspect lay beneath the surface. For, as the proverb says, *There is a great deal of unmapped country within us*. Such an activity – enabling people to grow – benefits the organization as well as the individual. Few things are more satisfying to a good leader.

Exercise

Can you think of three examples of people who have discovered that they had unsuspected but useful talents as a result of leaders taking an interest in what they could contribute, rather than focusing on what they couldn't do well?

Has this ever happened to you?

Creative leadership, then, is the kind that prospects for the greatness in each individual and then releases it. *Even in the coldest flint there is fire*. Often what people are hired to do doesn't turn out to be their *métier*. Your first job buys you a ticket into a vocational community; if you are lucky and encounter good leadership, the organization will work in partnership with you to ensure that you are making your maximum contribution.

Leadership has more to it, of course, than the giving of encouragement and opportunity. To be a leader is to accept that, to some extent, you are cast in the role of the demanding, hard-to-please Master in the Parable of the Talents, however you choose to play it. You will find yourself sometimes challenging others to be and do their best, for even common tasks make inexorable demands which must be met. As an Italian proverb says: 'By asking the impossible, you get the best possible.'

This may sound unreasonable, but, as George Bernard Shaw once remarked, 'Nothing is ever accomplished by a reasonable man.' Jan Leschly, then chief executive of one of the largest pharmaceutical companies in the world, once explained clearly what 'unreasonable' means in this context. 'If I think about my own life,' he said, 'the real big changes where I really learnt something, that was done by an unreasonable leader. I am not talking about being rude, about being nasty, about being unpleasant. I'm talking about unreasonable – asking for things that people say: "That's nearly impossible for us to do."'

'Many people die with the music still in them,' writes Oliver Wendell Holmes. As it is the function of the conductor to draw great music from the orchestra, so a leader's task is to evoke the talents of each 'player' in the team. 'Those who are near will not hide their ability, and those who are distant will not grumble at their toil,' wrote Hsun Tzu in ancient China. 'That is what is called being a leader and teacher of men.'

A leader should not set out to be popular nor even to be liked, though of course, it is unnatural to enjoy not being liked. Respect attends leaders who know their business, and affection usually flows in its train. The leader is there primarily to enable all to achieve the common task, however uphill the road. But in working with individuals – all leaders should have an equal-but-different relationship with each individual in the immediate team as well as with the team or organization as a whole – the good leader may be more a coach and consultant, even sometimes a mentor. Thereby a leader may often be the catalyst whereby others realize and bring unsuspected or hidden talents to market.

Demanding though he or she may be, the leader respects the other person – the team or individual – as an equal. They are always free to leave. The option is to go home, to take what Keats called 'that journey homewards to habitual self'.

Leadership that Evokes Greatness

Sir Neville Marriner, founder and principal conductor of the Academy of St Martin-in-the-Fields, once played in the London Symphony Orchestra:

> As a player, I was with the LSO, which has always been regarded as the second best orchestra in London. Then Stokowski was persuaded to come and work with the LSO and in about three days he managed to transmit to us the notion that we were a great orchestra. It gave us enormous confidence and we suddenly realised, in one concert at the Festival Hall, that we could achieve, had just achieved, a great performance – that we could achieve it just as easily as any other orchestra in the world. I think it was a great turning point for the orchestra suddenly to be given this confidence in one performance.
>
> From that moment the LSO never looked back – it was extraordinary. What did he do? He put more responsibility on the players than they had before. He more or less said to them, 'This is your orchestra and if you want it to be good then you must perform. I will do my best to make it happen but the responsibility is yours.' He just had this remarkable ability to focus the emotion of an entire orchestra. His personality was immensely strong.

Jan R. Jonassen, *Leadership: Sharing the Passion* (1999)

Shakespeare captured the challenging spirit of a true leader in King Henry V's speech before Agincourt. The English army was greatly outnumbered. 'He that has not stomach for this fight, *let him depart.*' Passport and money will be provided. But to those who choose to stay – now the king's equals, his 'brothers-in-arms' – Henry has this to say:

We few, we happy few, we band of brothers;
For he today that sheds his blood with me
Shall be my brother; be he ne'er so vile
This day shall gentle his condition.

Contrary to popular belief true leaders do not seek people to be their followers; they are more intent upon making people feel *partners* with them in the common enterprise.

Fortunately for us, there is no want of great challenges to evoke greatness, creativity and nobility from people. As the tectonic plates of change grind together they throw up hills and mountains of tasks, enough for countless millennia. And so good leaders – and leaders for good – will never want for employment. 'It is provided in the essence of things,' said Walt Whitman, 'that from any fraction of success, no matter what, shall come further something to make a great struggle necessary.'

Summary of Key Points

- Vocation is the matrix of true leadership. For vocational people tend to fulfil the first necessary condition for a leader, namely that they possess the characteristics admired in that field. They don't have a problem with credibility.
- Vocational people are often creative pioneers in their field, going into territory where no one has gone before. If they attract followers on the path that they blazon, then they find themselves – often to their surprise – being looked upon as leaders.
- In corporate or organizational life, the other side of the leadership coin – the ability to make everyone partners in the common enterprise – becomes equally important. Providing direction, leading by example, teambuilding and team-working, motivating and inspiring others, are integral to the role of leadership.
- The path of leadership is an inner one as well as an outer one. It is not to be undertaken lightly. 'The outward work

---

Checklist – Do you Have a Secondary Vocation for Leadership?

In the past year has anyone used the words leader or leadership to describe you?

Bearing in mind that leadership is service, do you still aspire to a leadership role?

Have you read any books on leadership or attended any leadership courses?

Is your temperament or personality such that you create harmony in groups rather than divisiveness?

Does it come naturally to you to be interested in other people, especially in their interests and aptitudes?

Have others described you as 'a good judge of character'?

Do you believe that people need stimulus and encouragement if they are to persevere in the journey of discovering and using the best that lies within them?

When you have been in a leadership role have you found it – in spite of the hassle – fundamentally enjoyable and personally rewarding?

---

can never be small,' wrote Meister Eckhart, the fourteenth-century mystic, 'if the inward one is great, and the outward work can never be great or good if the inward is small or of little worth. The inward work always includes in itself all size, all breadth and all length.'

- The Hourglass-shaped and the Inverted Funnel Models of Career Change (figure 8.1) give you two broad vocational paths. Stay as a specialist and seek excellence, or widen out as a generalist, as an organizational leader. If you take the second path, excellence remains your aim, but it is now excellence as a leader.

- Leaders, like orchestral conductors, are there to enable all the voices or instruments to be heard to their best effect in harmony. Their role as leaders within their specific fields is to identify, develop and use all the talents of their people in a creative symphony of service to the common good.

A leader is best,
When people are hardly aware of his existence,
Not so good when people praise his government,
Less good when people stand in fear,
Worst, when people are contemptuous.
Fail to honour people, and they will fail to honour you.
But a good leader, who speaks little,
When his task is accomplished, his work done,
The people say, 'We did it ourselves!'

Leo Tsze 7th century BC

Postscript

Who would true valour see
Let him come hither;
One here will constant be,
Come wind, come weather.
There's no discouragement
Shall make him once relent
His first avow'd intent
To be a pilgrim.

John Bunyan

There is a Japanese proverb which says: *The journey is also the destination.* The quest to find your vocation is actually part of your vocation. Or, putting it another way, your call to be a vocational person comes first, and then you find your vocation – your niche in life, the work you love to do – somewhere along the way.

That general commitment to the lifelong vocational aim – 'the first avow'd intent' – is one of those 'necessary conditions' which, I have suggested, you need to fulfil. Doing so will not guarantee that you find your vocation, but it will ensure that you deserve to do so.

Elsewhere in this book I have borrowed from the poets the metaphor of building an altar, one that will be lit by a flame from on high – the element that you cannot supply yourself. Call it inspiration, providence, or luck, it is the moment when things begin – at last! – to fall into place.

The word 'niche' comes from the French verb meaning to

nest, not something we associate with altars. Yet in the broad courts of the Temple in Jerusalem there stood stone altars under the sun and blue sky. One of the writers of the Psalms noticed one day that some irreverent birds had made their nests in the dry-stone walling of these altars: 'Even the sparrow finds a home, and the swallow a nest for herself, where she may lay her young, at your altars, O Lord.' Build your personal altar carefully, and the 'birds of the air' will, as it were, create your niche.

The journey is your destination, for in time it becomes your vocation. It is a slow transformational process, one that calls for your patience as well as your creativity. For it is more like painting a picture than trying to work out the answer to a difficult sum.

The beauty of it, the final blessing, is that the journey never ends. 'There is no stopping place in this life,' wrote Meister Eckhart. 'No, nor was there one for anyone – no matter how far along the way they've come. This then, above all things; be ready for the gifts of God and always for new ones.'

Thank you for keeping me company on our journey together, and for listening to what I have had to say. I trust that you will have gained as much from reading this book as I have from writing it, and that this blessing of vocation will come your way. Perhaps you will then be able to echo the words of the poet:

> . . . *I made no vows, but vows*
> *Were then made for me; bond unknown to me*
> *Was given, that I should be, else sinning greatly,*
> *A dedicated Spirit. On I walked*
> *In thankful blessedness, which yet survives.*